Using the Standards
Algebra

Grade 2

by
Claire Piddock

Published by Instructional Fair
an imprint of
Frank Schaffer Publications®

Instructional Fair

Author: Claire Piddock
Editor: Karen Thompson

Frank Schaffer Publications®

Instructional Fair is an imprint of Frank Schaffer Publications.

Send all inquiries to:
Frank Schaffer Publications
3195 Wilson Drive NW
Grand Rapids, Michigan 49534

Using the Standards: Algebra—grade 2

ISBN: 0-7424-2882-6

3 4 5 6 7 8 9 10 MAZ 10 09 08 07 06

Table of Contents

0-7424-2882-6 *Using the Standards—Algebra*

Introduction

Using the Standards—Algebra is designed to support and enhance student understanding of relationships among quantities, ways of representing those relationships, and concepts of change. Based on the National Council of Mathematics Teachers (NCTM) standards, this book builds upon and integrates a second-grade student's experience with numbers, geometric figures, and graphs. All activities can be done independently, in pairs, or in groups.

The pages in this book are organized according to the four NCTM Algebra Standards for grades K–2.

Understanding patterns, relations, and functions: In the **Patterns and Functions** section, students sort and order objects and numbers, they identify many kinds of patterns, including shape, number, and sound patterns, and they describe and extend them. Students also develop different ways to represent the same pattern and analyze how repeating and growing patterns come about.

Representing mathematical situations and structures using algebraic symbols: In the **Situations and Structures** section, students build upon their number knowledge to illustrate general principles through specific examples. They explore various ways to represent relationships such as equal to, greater than, and less than. In these early grades, students build toward the later use of conventional algebraic symbols by describing mathematical situations using words, objects, drawings, and their own invented symbols.

Using mathematical models to represent and understand quantitative relationships: The **Models** section zeroes in on concepts of addition and subtraction, using multiple ways to depict the situations. Students study problems, interpret and draw pictures, and manipulate objects, as well as use conventional symbols to express addition and subtraction.

Analyze changes in various contexts: The **Changes in Context** section focuses on qualitative change and quantitative change. Students recognize and describe changes over time that can be expressed without numbers (qualitative). They identify and describe changes that can be expressed using numbers (quantitative) and assign numbers appropriately.

0-7424-2882-6 *Using the Standards—Algebra*

Introduction (cont.)

Every one of the 100+ activities, while focused on the algebra content standard, also incorporates one or more of the five NCTM process standards:

 Problem Solving—building and applying knowledge through solving problems set in many contexts, using appropriate strategies.

 Reasoning and Proof—making and investigating conjectures and developing ways to reason about mathematical situations and to evaluate others' reasoning.

 Communication—organizing and expressing mathematical ideas verbally in everyday language and in precise mathematical language.

 Connections—recognizing and using connections among mathematical ideas and applying mathematics in other contexts.

Representation—select, create, organize, use, and apply various ways to represent mathematical ideas or to interpret situations.

Other Features:

Think and **Do More** prompts at the end of each activity encourage students to speak and write about content objectives and their problem-solving strategies or to extend their skills. They can be used as journal prompts, class discussions, or pair-share questions.

Pretest and **Posttest** sections are included for evaluations. Teachers may use the pretest to determine areas that need emphasis. The posttest can be used for assessment or for extra practice.

Check Your Skills pages at the end of each content section allow for monitoring of progress or can be used for extra practice.

Vocabulary Cards can be cut and pasted on index cards and used for flash cards or math games.

Create Your Own Problems pages provide a unique opportunity to assess students' understanding and to prepare students for constructed response questions on standardized tests. Follow these and other open-ended questions within these activities with classroom discussions and evaluation of responses. Scoring guides can help you analyze students' responses and help students judge their own progress. The following is one possible scoring rubric. Modify this rubric as necessary to fit specific problems.

1—Student understands the problem and knows what he/she is being asked to find.
2—Student selects an appropriate strategy or process to solve the problem.
3—Student is able to model the problem with appropriate symbols, pictures, graphs, tables, computations, or number sentences.
4—Student is able to clearly explain or demonstrate his/her thinking and reasoning.

5

NCTM Algebra Standards Correlation Chart

	Problem Solving	Reasoning and Proof	Communication	Connections	Representation
Patterns and Functions					
sort and classify	11, 14, 15, 18	9, 10, 11, 19, 40, 41	14, 18	14, 15, 16, 17, 19, 41	10, 16, 17, 40, 41
recognize, describe and extend patterns	13, 22	13	12, 21, 24, 26, 31	12, 24, 26, 29, 31, 32, 37	20, 21, 28, 29, 30, 37
repeating and growing patterns	23, 25, 33, 38, 39	39, 42, 43	27, 36, 38	27, 33, 34, 35, 36, 42	23, 34, 35, 43
Situations and Structures					
identify and use properties	48, 49	46, 47, 50, 51, 54	47, 51, 52, 56	46, 52, 53, 54, 55, 56	48, 54, 55
symbolic notations	57, 59, 60, 62, 63, 64, 65, 66, 67	57, 62, 63, 64, 65	21, 57, 58	61, 66, 67	20, 21, 58, 59, 61, 64, 65, 66
Models					
model situations involving whole numbers	75, 76, 77, 79, 80, 81		74, 75, 77	70, 71, 74, 75, 76, 78, 79, 80, 81	70, 71, 72, 73, 77, 78, 79, 80, 81
Changes in Context					
qualitive change	88	89, 90	85, 86, 87, 90	84, 85, 86, 87, 88	88, 89
quantitive change	93, 94, 96, 97, 98, 101, 104	98, 100, 105, 106	91, 92, 93, 99	91, 92, 93, 94, 95, 96, 97, 99, 100, 101, 102, 103, 104	102, 103, 104, 105, 106

*The pretest, posttest, Create Your Own Problems, and Check Your Skills pages are not included on this chart, but contain a representative sampling of the process standards.

0-7424-2882-6 *Using the Standards—Algebra*

Pretest

1. Study the pattern.

   a. Describe the pattern in words.

   b. Circle the kind of pattern.   **growing**   **repeating**

   c. Draw the next shape in the pattern.

2. Study the numbers.

   a. Write the numbers on the cards in order from least to greatest.

   _____   _____   _____   _____   _____   _____

   b. Write the next number in the pattern. _____

3. Sort the objects.

   a. Make two groups. Circle the things that belong together.

   b. Describe how you sorted.

4. Describe the rule for sorting these cards.

8	26	33	30	17	14	25

5. Draw the next two shapes. □ □ ○ ○ □ □ ○ ○ □

6. Show how you can group the numbers to make these additions easier. Use ( ).
Then solve the problems.

   a. 8 + 2 + 9 = _____   **b.** 54 + 30 + 70 = _____

7

Pretest (cont.)

7. Which example shows the order property of addition? Circle it.

a. $8 + 10 = 10 + 8$ **b.** $7 + 0 = 7$ **c.** $(7 + 8) + 5 = 7 + (8 + 5)$

8. Write >, <, or = to make each sentence true.

a. $91 \bigcirc 19$ **b.** $4 + 8 \bigcirc 10 + 4$

9. Look at the picture. Circle the correct comparison word.

a. Megan is **taller shorter** than Asia.

b. Megan has **longer shorter** hair than Asia.

Megan   Asia

10. Write the number that makes the sentence true. $25 + \square = 31$

11. Find three numbers that make the sentence true. $10 > 3 + \square$

_____ _____ _____

12. Find the value of $\square$. Explain how you know. $\square + \square + 2 = 10$

13. Write a fact family using these three numbers.   9   16   7

14. Fill in the table to show the change from IN numbers to OUT numbers.

IN	1	2	3	4	5
OUT	8	9	10		

0-7424-2882-6 *Using the Standards—Algebra*

Name _____ Date _____

What Belongs?

Directions: Look at the picture. Write the word on the correct row.

dog   ball   rope   bird

game   hamburger   cat   candy   banana

1. Pets:

_____ _____ _____

2. Toys:

_____ _____ _____

3. Food:

_____ _____ _____

4. Write one more thing that belongs in each group.

5. Name three things that belong to the following group.

   School things:

   _____ _____ _____

DO MORE

Tell how you chose the things that belong in each group.

0-7424-2882-6 *Using the Standards—Algebra*

Name _____ Date _____

Sort and Graph

Directions: Look at the foods. How can you sort them?

1. Sort. Use tally marks.

   a. Fruit _____

   b. Grains _____

   c. Meat _____

   d. Vegetables _____

2. Make a graph.

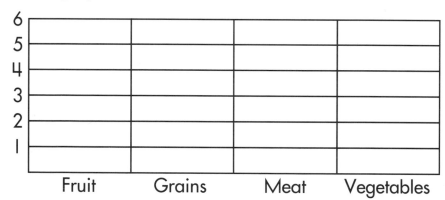

3. Write the number in each group in order from most to least.

   _____ _____ _____ _____

DO MORE

Think of another way you might sort the foods. What rule would you use?

10

Name _____ Date _____

Alphabet Soup

Directions: Carla, Billy, and Pedro eat alphabet soup. They each like different flavors. Sort the letters to find what goes into each person's bowl.

1. Carla likes only carrots. The letters shaded like C taste like carrots. Write her letters in the bowl. How many does she get? _____

2. Billy likes only beets. The letters shaded like **H** taste like beets. Write his letters in the bowl. How many does he get? _____

3. Pedro likes only peas. The letters shaded like **D** taste like peas. Write his letters in the bowl. How many does he get? _____

THINK

Think of two more ways in which you might sort the letters. Describe your sorting rule.

0-7424-2882-6 *Using the Standards—Algebra*

Name _____ Date _____

Pattern Blocks

Directions: Use pattern blocks to make patterns. Answer questions about what you make.

I.

a. How many different shapes did you use? _____ Draw the shapes.

b. What order did you use? _____

c. Describe what you did to make the pattern.

d. Continue the pattern. Draw what the next block will be.

e. How can you find out what the tenth block is?

f. Draw the tenth block.

2. Use blocks to make your own pattern. Draw it here.

DO MORE

Look around. Where can you find patterns like these?

0-7424-2882-6 *Using the Standards—Algebra*

Name _____ Date _____

Order It

Directions: Tia is at the beach. She lines up her things by her blanket when she goes into the water. Find the correct order.

Her sandals are not first.

Her drink is third.

Her towel is next to her drink.

Her sun block is before the towel.

1. Which thing can you put in its place first? _____

2. The sandals are not first. Where could they be? _____

3. Where could the towel be? _____

4. Write the things in order.

   _____ _____ _____ _____

5. Explain how you decided on the final order.

THINK

What helped you the most to figure out this puzzle?

0-7424-2882-6 *Using the Standards—Algebra*

Name _____ Date _____

Sorting Blocks

Directions: Sort blocks. Find three different ways to sort. Circle the shapes that belong together.

I.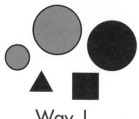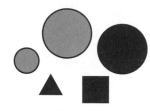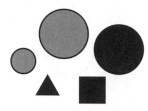

Way 1   Way 2   Way 3

2. Describe how you sort each group of blocks.

    a. Way 1 _____

    b. Way 2 _____

    c. Way 3 _____

3.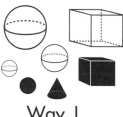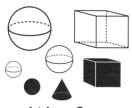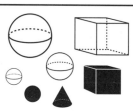

Way 1   Way 2   Way 3

4. Describe how you sort each group of blocks.

    a. Way 1 _____

    b. Way 2 _____

    c. Way 3 _____

DO MORE

Use attribute blocks. Take any 9 blocks with your eyes closed. Sort the blocks in three different ways. Describe the ways to a partner.

14

Name _____ Date _____

Sorting Buttons

Directions: The buttons fell out of Mrs. Taylor's box. Help her pick them up and sort them.

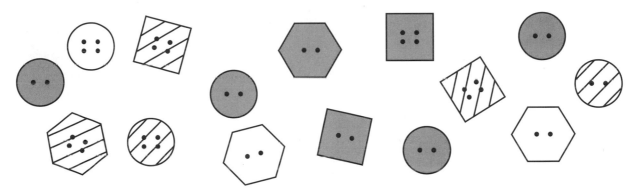

1. Sort by shape. Write the number.

circles

squares

hexagons

_____ _____ _____

2. Sort by shade and design. Write the number.

grey

white

striped

_____ _____ _____

3. Use sorting buttons or play coins. Sort them in as many ways as you can.

THINK

In what other way can you sort the buttons?

0-7424-2882-6 *Using the Standards—Algebra*

Name _____ Date _____

Animal Babies

Directions: Count the babies each animal has. Write the number. Then compare.

1.  _____

2.  _____

3.  _____

4. _____

5. Circle the animal above that has the most babies.

6. Use a graph to compare numbers. Color one block for each baby animal.

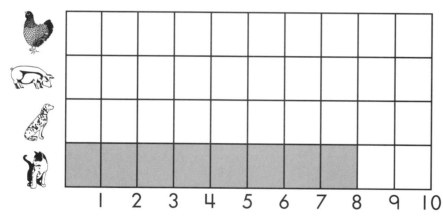

7. Write the number of animal babies in order from least to greatest.

_____ _____ _____ _____

8. How does the graph help you see order? _____

DO MORE

How many more chicks would the hen need to have the most babies? Describe how you find your answer.

0-7424-2882-6 *Using the Standards—Algebra*

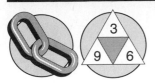

Name _____ Date _____

Weather Wise

Directions: Look at the weather chart for weekdays in February. What kind of
weather do you see? How can you tell someone about the weather?

	Monday	Tuesday	Wednesday	Thursday	Friday
Week 1	cloud 2	cloud 3	cloud 4	rain 5	sun 6
Week 2	cloud 9	sun 10	sun 11	cloud 12	snow 13
Week 3	rain 16	snow 17	sun 18	rain 19	snow 20
Week 4	cloud 23	sun 24	cloud 25	rain 26	sun 27

1. Sort the number of sunny, cloudy, rainy, and snowy days.

    a. How many sunny days? ☼ _____   **b.** How many cloudy days? ☁ _____
    c. How many rainy days? 🌧 _____   **d.** How many snowy days? ❄ _____

2. Write the numbers in order from least to greatest.

    _____ _____ _____

3. Sort another way to compare the weather on Thursdays.

    a. How many sunny days? ☼ _____   **b.** How many cloudy days? ☁ _____
    c. How many rainy days? 🌧 _____   **d.** How many snowy days? ❄ _____

4. Write the numbers in order from least to greatest.
    a. _____ _____ _____
    b. Why can you write only three numbers?

DO MORE

Make a bar graph using this data or weather data that you collect.

0-7424-2882-6 *Using the Standards—Algebra*

Name _____ Date _____

Comparing Numbers

Comparison signs help you write math sentences about order.

> means **is greater than**   < means **is less than**   = means **is equal to**

Directions: Use the comparison signs to answer the questions.

1.   Write the sign. Write the words under it.

   a. 38 _____ 40   **b.** 23 + 7 _____ 30   **c.** 34 + 8 _____ 40

   _____   _____   _____

   d. 14 _____ 64   **e.** 51 + 7 _____ 61   **f.** 100 – 10 _____ 80 + 10

   _____   _____   _____

2.   Play a game with number cubes.
      Toss two cubes. Write as many math
      sentences as you can using comparison signs.

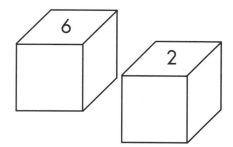

   a. First toss

   b. Second toss

   c. When can you write only once math sentence?

THINK

Explain why the equal sign is called a comparison sign.

0-7424-2882-6 *Using the Standards—Algebra*

Name _____ Date _____

Pennies and Nickels

Directions: Figure it out. Find out what coins each person has. Then find who has more money. Use coins or counters if needed.

Madison has 3 more pennies than nickels.

Casey has 2 more nickels than Madison.

Madison has 3 nickels.

Casey has 5 pennies.

Hint: You can write N for nickel and P for penny as you give it to Madison or Casey. Then you can cross off each coin as you give it to Madison or Casey.

1. Which coins does Madison have?

2. Which coins does Casey have?

3. How much money does Madison have? _____ cents

4. How much money does Casey have? _____ cents

5. Use >, <, or = to compare the amounts of money. Write two math sentences.

a. _____ **b.** _____

DO MORE

Imagine you have 7 nickels. Write your name along with Casey's and Madison's in the order from the greatest to the least amount of money.

0-7424-2882-6 *Using the Standards—Algebra*

Name _____ Date _____

Puzzles

Directions: In these puzzles, each number stands for a letter. Follow the directions to find the answer to each question.

1. Emily loves to do this. What is it?

A = 20   C = 40   D = 10   E = 50   N = 30

Write the numbers in order from least to greatest. Then write their matching letters in the same order.

_____ _____ _____ _____ _____

_____ _____ _____ _____ _____

2. Roberto was happy about a math test. Why?

A = 18   K = 22   M = 16   O = 12   P = 14   R = 20   T = 10

Write the numbers in order from least to greatest. Then write their matching letters in the same order.

_____ _____ _____

_____ _____ _____ _____

_____ _____ _____

_____ _____ _____ _____

THINK

How are the numbers in these two puzzles alike?

0-7424-2882-6 *Using the Standards—Algebra*

Name _____ Date _____

More Puzzles

1. The Garcia family takes two trips. When?

A = 29   C = 19   H = 12   J = 9

L = 5   M = 30   R = 28   U = 8   Y = 3

Write the numbers in order from greatest to least. Then write their matching letters in the same order.

_____ _____ _____ _____ _____

_____ _____ _____ _____

_____ _____ _____ _____

_____ _____ _____

2. How is the code in problem 3 different from other codes?

3. Make up a number-letter puzzle like the one on this page. Use it to write a message for a friend to figure out.

THINK

Explain why a puzzle based on a number pattern is easier to figure out than one that is not based on a pattern.

0-7424-2882-6 *Using the Standards—Algebra*

Name _____ Date _____

Toy Shelf

Directions: Donita arranges her toys in patterns. Look at the order of the objects to find the patterns.

1. 🚗 🚗 🚗 🚗 _____

Circle what comes next. 🚗 🚗

Describe the pattern.

2. 🐻 🐱 🐰 🐻 _____ 🐰 🐻 🐱

Circle the missing one. 🐻 🐱 🐰

Describe the pattern.

3.

Two things are missing. Circle what goes in space A.

Circle what goes in space B. ⛵ Soccer

Describe the pattern.

DO MORE

Use two or more shapes like these to make two different patterns.

0-7424-2882-6 *Using the Standards—Algebra*

Name _____ Date _____

Linking Patterns

Jacob made a **repeating** pattern.

Directions: Use Learning Links, colored cubes, or colored paper clips. Make patterns with colors. Color the spaces below to show your pattern.

1. Choose any two colors.

   a. Make a repeating pattern.

   b. Make a different repeating pattern using the same two colors.

   c. How are your two patterns different? Describe what you did.

2. Choose any three colors.

   a. Make a repeating pattern.

   b. Describe your pattern.

THINK

Here is a repeating number pattern: 1 2 3 1 2 3 1
Tell how the pattern is the same or different from your pattern using three colors.

0-7424-2882-6 *Using the Standards—Algebra*

Name _____ Date _____

Sound It Out

Directions: Music has lots of patterns. Imagine this rhythm band. Look at the patterns.

Draw the missing  or .

1.  _____

2.   _____

3. _____       _____

4.   _____    _____

5. Choose one of the patterns. Describe the pattern. Tell how you figured it out.

DO MORE

Make up two of your own patterns using the   and .

0-7424-2882-6 *Using the Standards—Algebra*

Name _____ Date _____

Shape Up

Directions: Draw the shape that comes next in each row. Answer the questions.

1.   _____

2.    _____

3. In the two patterns above, two different shapes repeat. Draw a pattern in which two shapes repeat.

4. Draw a pattern in which three different shapes repeat.

5.   _____

What changes in this pattern? _____

6.   _____

What changes in this pattern? _____

DO MORE

Draw your own pattern. Change the size and shape. Make another pattern. Change the shape and color.

 0-7424-2882-6 *Using the Standards—Algebra*

Name _____ Date _____

Patterns in Rows

Directions: Describe the patterns. What comes next? Continue the patterns by coloring the boxes.

1. Row 1

Row 2

a. Describe the pattern you see in the first row.

b. Describe the pattern you see in the second row.

c. Continue the pattern.

2. Row 1

Row 2

Row 3

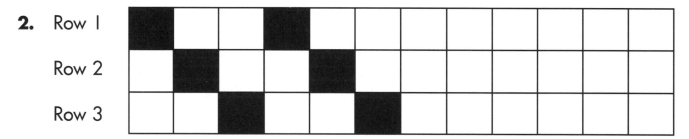

a. Describe the pattern your way.

b. Continue the pattern.

THINK

Where might you see patterns like these?

0-7424-2882-6 *Using the Standards—Algebra*

Name _____ Date _____

Make a Quilt

Directions: This pattern goes two ways. Describe it in many ways. Finish coloring to make the quilt.

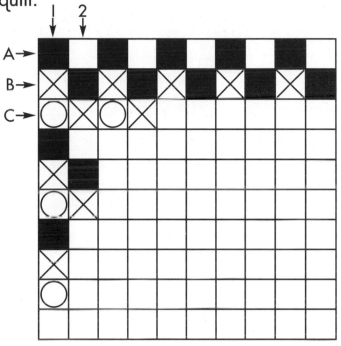

1. Describe the pattern in row A. _____

2. Describe the pattern in row B. _____

3. Describe the pattern in row C. _____

4. Describe the pattern in column 1. _____

5. Describe the pattern in column 2. _____

6. Color to finish the quilt.

DO MORE

Use grid paper to design your own quilt patterns.

0-7424-2882-6 *Using the Standards—Algebra*

Name _____ Date _____

Different Ways

Directions: Draw the next shapes in each row. Answer the questions.

1.  _____ _____

2. _____ _____

3. _____ _____

4.  _____ _____ _____

5. You can show a pattern in different ways. These patterns are the same.

A   B   A   B   A   B

1   2   1   2   1   2

a. Use the letters A and B to show the same pattern as in question 1 above.

_____

b. Use the numbers 4 and 5 to show the same pattern as in question 2 above.

_____

c. Use letters or numbers to show the same pattern as in question 3 above.

_____

THINK

How many different letters do you need to show the pattern in example 4 above? Write the pattern using letters.

0-7424-2882-6 *Using the Standards—Algebra*

Name _____ Date _____

Old MacDonald

Directions: Do you know this song? The first line says "Old MacDonald had a farm E I E I O."

1. The letters E I E I O make a pattern. Use the letters to extend the pattern.
   E I E I O ____ ____ ____ ____ ____

2. Use numbers to make the same pattern.
   a. What number will you use in place of the letter E?   _____
   b. What number will you use in place of the letter I?   _____
   c. What number will you use in place of the letter O?   _____
   d. Write the matching pattern.

   ___ ___ ___ ___ ___ ___ ___ ___ ___ ___

3. Part of the song says "oink oink here, oink oink there." Repeat those words to make a pattern. Fill in the words.

   oink oink _____ oink oink _____ oink oink _____ oink oink _____

4. Use numbers to make the same pattern.
   a. What number will you use in place of the word *oink*?   _____
   b. What number will you use in place of the word *here*?   _____
   c. What number will you use in place of the word *there*? _____
   d. Write the matching pattern.

   ___ ___ ___ ___ ___ ___ ___ ___ ___

THINK

Suppose someone has never heard the song. Explain how the song uses patterns to make it fun and interesting.

0-7424-2882-6 *Using the Standards—Algebra*

Name _____ Date _____

Match Up

Directions: Find the patterns that match. Write the matching letter on the line.

_____ 1. A A B A A B

a. △ △ △ △ △ △

_____ 2. ☺ ☹ ☺ ☹ ☺

b. ♥ ↑ ↑ ↓ ↓ ↓ ● ● ● ●

_____ 3. ■ ▮ ● ■ ▮ ●

c. 2 2 8 2 2 8 2 2 8

_____ 4. 1 2 2 3 3 3 4 4 4

d. ↑ ↑ ↑ ↓ ↑ ↑ ↑ ↓

_____ 5. ● ● ● ○ ● ● ● ○

e. Q R S Q R S Q

DO MORE

Choose one of the patterns. Make 2 more matching patterns.

0-7424-2882-6 *Using the Standards—Algebra*

Name _____ Date _____

Pattern Search

> The **sum** is the answer to an addition problem.
> The **difference** is the answer to a subtraction problem.

Directions: Look for patterns in the answers. For letter **d** in each row, write an example to continue the pattern.

1. Add. Look for a pattern in the sums.

   a. 7
       + 4

   b. 8
       + 4

   c. 9
       + 4

   d.

   e. Describe the pattern of sums.

2. Subtract. Look for a pattern in the differences.

   a. 78
       − 10

   b. 78
       − 20

   c. 78
       − 30

   d.

   e. Describe the pattern of differences.

3. Look for a pattern. Write the next example to continue the pattern.

   a. 9
       + 8

   b. 8
       + 7

   c. 7
       + 6

   d.

   e. Describe the pattern.

DO MORE

Write four addition examples where the sums make a pattern of + 2.

0-7424-2882-6 *Using the Standards—Algebra*

Name _____ Date _____

Evens and Odds

An **even** number of objects can be grouped in 2s with none left over. 8 is an even number.

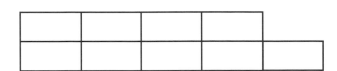

An **odd** number of objects has one left over when you group into 2s. 9 is an odd number.

Directions: Use linking cubes if you need help.

1. Write **even** or **odd** for each number.

   a. 12 _____   **b.** 35 _____   **c.** 41 _____

   d. 27 _____   **e.** 30 _____   **f.** 28 _____

> You can use a shortcut to find even and odd numbers.
> Even numbers end with 0, 2, 4, 6, or 8.
> Odd numbers end with 1, 3, 5, 7, or 9.

2. 79, 86, 98, 100, 67, 193

   Look at the street addresses. Even numbers go on the left side of the street. Odd numbers go on the right side of the street. Write the numbers in order and on the side of the street where they belong.

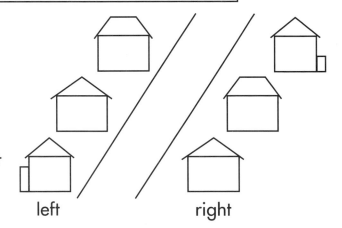

left   right

THINK

Imagine that you deliver newspapers to the houses. Start at the lowest house number. Describe the order in which you will go to the houses. Don't forget to tell when you have to cross the street.

0-7424-2882-6 *Using the Standards—Algebra*

Name _____ Date _____

Growing Money

Directions: Grandma puts money away each week for Nikki and Sean. Look at the banks to find out how much. Find out how the money grows.

1. Nikki

$1 $3 $5 $7 $ $ $ $

   a. By how much does Nikki's money grow each week? $ _____

   b. Describe the pattern in words.

   c. Write numbers on the banks to continue the pattern.

   d. How much will Nikki have in week 6? $ _____

Nikki's money shows a **growing** pattern. It grows by the **same amount** each week.

2. Sean

$1 $2 $4 $7 $ $ $ $

   a. By how much does Sean's money grow between week 1 and week 2? $____

   b. How much does it grow between week 2 and week 3? _____

   c. Look for a pattern. Describe the pattern in words.

   d. Write numbers on the banks to continue the pattern.

   e. How much will Sean have in week 6? $ _____

Sean's money is also a **growing** pattern. It grows by a **different amount** each week.

THINK

Will Nikki or Sean have more money at the end of the month? Explain how you know.

    0-7424-2882-6 *Using the Standards—Algebra*

Name _____ Date _____

Pictograph Patterns

Directions: Three children played a game to win tokens. Read the pictograph to see how many tokens they earned. What pattern do you see?

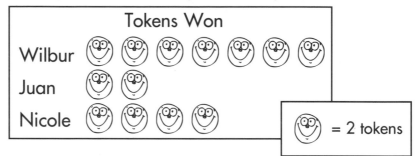

Tokens Won

Wilbur

Juan

Nicole

= 2 tokens

1. Count ☺ s.

  a. How many ☺ s are next to Wilbur's name? _____
  How many tokens did he win? _____

  b. How many ☺ s are next to Juan's name? _____
  How many tokens did he win? _____

  c. How many ☺ s are next to Nicole's name? _____
  How many tokens did she win? _____

2. What pattern helps you find the number of tokens each child won?

3. Draw 10 smiley faces below. Write the pattern below.

   2 4   ____ ____ ____ ____ ____ ____ ____ ____

THINK

Three children win 30, 15, and 10 tokens. What pattern could help you make the pictograph? Explain what each ☺ should equal to make the pictograph and why you chose it.

0-7424-2882-6 *Using the Standards—Algebra*

Name _____ Date _____

Skip Along

Directions: Skip counting makes patterns. Count forward or backward. Show the hops on the number line. Then write the pattern.

Count forward.

1. Count by 2s.

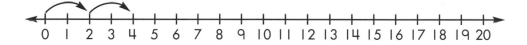

_____

2. Count by 3s.

_____

3. Count by 4s.

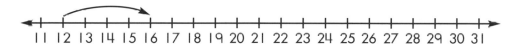

_____

Count backward.

4. Count back by 5s.

_____

5. Count back by 10s.

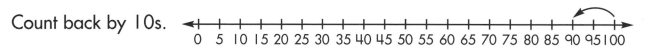

_____

THINK

How is the following pattern like the one in question 5? How is it different? Write the next two numbers.

123 113 103 93 _____ _____

0-7424-2882-6 *Using the Standards—Algebra*

Name _____   Date _____

Hot or Cold?

Directions: Read the temperatures on the graphs. Look for **growing** patterns.

1.

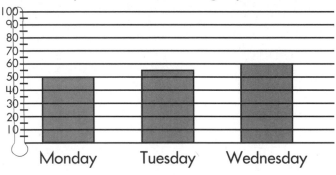

a. Read the temperatures.

Monday _____   Tuesday _____   Wednesday _____

b. Write the numbers as a pattern. Write 3 more numbers.

_____   _____   _____   _____   _____   _____

c. Is it a growing pattern? How do you know? _____

2.   Look at the two graphs.

a.

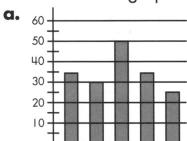

Describe the temperature changes.
Is this a growing pattern? Explain.

b.

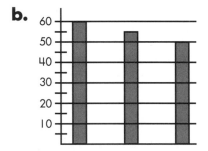

Describe the temperature changes.
Is this a growing pattern? Explain.

THINK

If the weather pattern in problem 2b continues, on what day will the temperature go below 32 degrees?

0-7424-2882-6 *Using the Standards—Algebra*

Name _____ Date _____

Hiding in Hundreds

Directions: Color the boxes. Find the patterns in the hundred chart.

1. Find the number 10. Color the box with 10 in it and all the boxes in its column. What numbers did you color? Write the number pattern.

1	2	3	4	5	6	7	8	9	10
11	12	13	14	15	16	17	18	19	20
21	22	23	24	25	26	27	28	29	30
31	32	33	34	35	36	37	38	39	40
41	42	43	44	45	46	47	48	49	50
51	52	53	54	55	56	57	58	59	60
61	62	63	64	65	66	67	68	69	70
71	72	73	74	75	76	77	78	79	80
81	82	83	84	85	86	87	88	89	90
91	92	93	94	95	96	97	98	99	100

2. Find the number 5. Color the box with the 5 in it and all the boxes in its column. What numbers did you color? Write the number pattern.

3. Find the number 3. Color the box with the 3 in it and all the boxes in its column. What numbers did you color? Write the number pattern.

4. How are the patterns in questions 1, 2, and 4 alike?

5. How are the patterns in questions 1, 2, and 4 different?

THINK

How can you find other **adding 10** patterns on the hundred chart?

0-7424-2882-6 *Using the Standards—Algebra*

Name _____ Date _____

Paint Set Patterns

Directions: A factory worker fills these paint sets.

1. Fill in the table to show how many there are after each new paint set is filled.

	1 set	2 sets	3 sets	4 sets	5 sets
Sketch pads	1				
Pencils	2				
Brushes	3				
Paint Jars	4				

2. Write the patterns.

Pads _____ _____ _____ _____ _____

Pencils _____ _____ _____ _____ _____

Brushes _____ _____ _____ _____ _____

Paint Jars _____ _____ _____ _____ _____

3. What is the same about all of the patterns? _____

4. What is different about the patterns? _____

5. Circle the number in the pattern that tells how many brushes there are in 4 paint sets.

DO MORE

Dante buys painting paper in sets of 5. Make up a story about Dante's paper that will result in a pattern about fives.

0-7424-2882-6 *Using the Standards—Algebra*

Name _____   Date _____

Bubbles, Bubbles, Everywhere

Directions: Here is a new video game. Every time you hit a bubble, it breaks into 2 more bubbles. You start with 1 bubble. You hit every bubble you try for. Draw a picture to see how fast your bubbles increase. The first few are done for you.

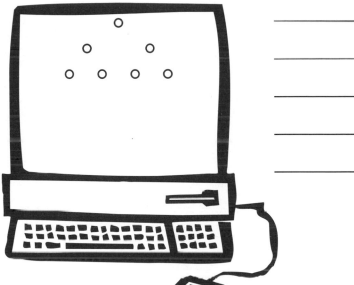

_____
_____
_____
_____
_____

1. Draw another two rows of bubbles.

2. Count the bubbles in each row. Write the numbers on the lines.

a. Is this a growing pattern? _____

b. Describe how the pattern is created. _____

c. Write the numbers in a pattern. Continue the pattern. Write two more numbers.

_____ _____ _____ _____ _____ _____

DO MORE

Add the bubbles one row at a time. You win the game when you reach 100 or more bubbles in all. In which row do you win the game?

Published by Instructional Fair. Copyright protected.   0-7424-2882-6 *Using the Standards—Algebra*

Name _____ Date _____

Ladybug Diagram

Directions: The ladybugs sit in different places. How are they sorted?

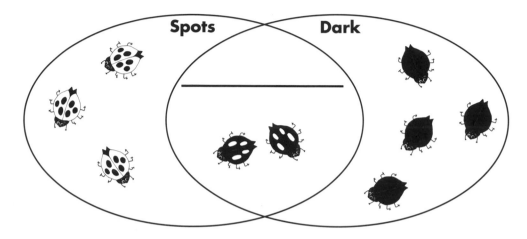

1. Write the number.

   a. _____ ladybugs have spots.

   b. _____ ladybugs are dark.

   c. _____ ladybugs are dark **and** have spots.

2. The circle on the left is labeled **Spots**. The circle on the right is labeled **Dark**.

   What should the place where the two circles overlap be called? _____

   Write your words on the line in the diagram.

THINK

What would go in the middle
of this diagram?

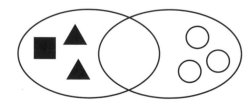

40

Name _____ Date _____

Music Diagram

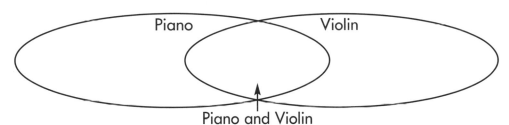

Piano   Violin

Piano and Violin

Directions: Read about the lessons the children take. Answer the questions. Put each name or number in the correct place in each diagram.

1. Savion, Elsa, and Marie take piano lessons. Marie and Joshua take violin lessons.
   a. Who takes piano and violin lessons? _____
   b. Who takes piano only? _____
   c. Who takes violin only? _____

2. Write the number.
   a. How many children take piano and violin? _____
   b. How many children take piano only? _____
   c. How many children take violin only? _____

3. Use these facts to write the numbers in the correct box.
   4 children take flute lessons.
   3 children take guitar lessons.
   2 children take flute and guitar lessons.

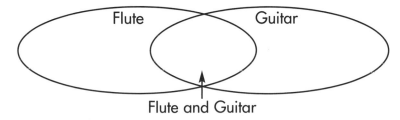

Flute   Guitar

Flute and Guitar

THINK

Sort attribute blocks. Use yarn or sorting circles for your two overlapping circles. Have a friend guess what your circles should be named.

0-7424-2882-6 *Using the Standards—Algebra*

Name _____ Date _____

Pizza Patterns

Directions: Olivia and Matt love pizza. They make a pizza with 6 slices. What does their pizza look like?

1. Olivia loves olives. She puts 1 olive on the first slice of pizza. She increases the number of olives on each slice. She adds 2 extra olives to each slice.

Add olives to the pizza picture.

a. How many olives are on the sixth slice? _____

b. What number pattern shows what Olivia did?

1, 3, _____, _____, _____, _____

2. Matt loves meatballs. He puts 1 meatball on the first slice. He increases the number of meatballs on each slice. He adds 3 extra meatballs on each slice.

Add meatballs to the pizza picture.

a. How many meatballs are on the sixth slice? _____

b. What number pattern shows what Matt did?

1, 4, _____, _____, _____, _____

DO MORE

Describe how you would find the total number of meatballs and olives on the pizza. Find the total.

Published by Instructional Fair. Copyright protected.

0-7424-2882-6 *Using the Standards—Algebra*

Name _____ Date _____

Up and Down

Directions: Follow the directions to make patterns going up and down the ladder. Use your fingers to do the climbing.

1. Start at 2.
   a. Climb up 4 steps. Where are you? Write the number.
   b. Climb down 1 step. Where are you? Write the number.
   c. Now go back up 4 steps. Where are you? Write the number.
   d. Climb back down 1 step. Where are you? Write the number.
   e. Repeat one more time. Climb up 4.
       Then climb down 1.

2. Write the numbers above in the order you found them.

   2, _____, _____, _____, _____, _____, _____

   You have made a pattern.

   You can describe the pattern using addition and subtraction. Add 4. Then subtract 1.

3. Use the ladder to help you find this pattern. Begin at 5.
   Add 7. Then subtract 3.
   Write six numbers in the pattern.

   5, _____, _____, _____, _____, _____, _____

4. Make up your own pattern that uses addition and subtraction.
   Write the rule below. Then write six numbers in the pattern.
   Your rule: _____
   Pattern: _____ _____ _____ _____ _____ _____

20
19
18
17
16
15
14
13
12
11
10
9
8
7
6
5
4
3
2
1

DO MORE

Don't give away your rule. Have a friend try to figure out how you made your pattern.

Published by Instructional Fair. Copyright protected. 0-7424-2882-6 *Using the Standards—Algebra*

Name _____ Date _____

Create Your Own Problems

1. Find out the birthday—month, day, and year—of four friends. Include your birthday, too.

    a. Find two different ways you can order the information.

    b. Make up a rule for sorting the information.

2. Create a repeating pattern with shapes and a matching pattern with numbers.

3. Write a rule for sorting the letters of the alphabet.

4. Give directions for finding a pattern on a hundred chart.

5. Use numbers. Make up a growing pattern. Then make up a decreasing pattern.

6. Draw a number line to show a pattern using even numbers.

0-7424-2882-6 *Using the Standards—Algebra*

Name _____ Date _____

Check Your Skills

I. Write the numbers from greatest to least. 142   42   34   103   131

_____   _____   _____   _____   _____

2. Fill in the blank with >, <, or =.   **a.** 89 _____ 79   **b.** 100 + 14 _____ 114

3. Which shows sets sorted correctly?

a. set 1 △ △ □   set 2 □ □ □ □

b. set 1 ⊘ ⊘   set 2 ○ ○   set 3 ⊗ ⊗ ⊗

4. Draw the next two shapes in the pattern.

● ♥ ● ♥ ● ♥ ♥ ♥ ♥

5. Write the next two numbers in each pattern. Then write **growing** or **repeating**.

a. 5 8 11 14 17 ____ ____   _____

b. 5 8 11 5 8 ____ ____   _____

7. Use the letters A, B, and C to write a matching pattern.

4 4 2 3 4 4 2 3 _____

8. Write **growing** or **repeating** for each pattern.

_____ **a.** Isabella puts $1.75 a week into her bank.

_____ **b.** ☀ ☁ ☁ ☀ ☁ ☁ ☀

_____ **c.** The numbers you get when you count by fives.

45

Name _____ Date _____

Order in Your Life

Directions: Think about the following events. Does order matter?

1. You get dressed.
    You put on your socks first. Then you put on your shoes.
    You put on your shoes first. Then you put on your socks.
    a. Does order matter? _____
    b. Explain your thinking.

2. You pay for gum with a quarter and a dime.
    You give a quarter first and then a dime.
    You give a dime first and then a quarter.
    a. Does order matter? _____
    b. Explain your thinking.

3. You have two slices of bread to make a peanut butter and jelly sandwich.
    You spread the peanut butter first. Then you spread the jelly.
    You spread the jelly first. Then you spread the peanut butter.
    a. Does order matter? _____
    b. Explain your thinking.

4. Your mom cooks a boiled egg.
    She breaks the egg shell. Then she boils it.
    She boils the egg. Then she breaks the egg shell.
    a. Does order matter? _____
    b. Explain your thinking.

DO MORE

Give an example of a time when order does not matter. Can you think of a math example?

0-7424-2882-6 *Using the Standards—Algebra*

Name _____ Date _____

Order in Addition

$$30 + 5 = 40 \leftarrow \textbf{sum}$$
$$\uparrow \qquad \uparrow$$
$$\textbf{addends}$$

Directions: Study the addition problems. Does order matter?

1. Add two ways.

a. 6 + 8 = _____   8 + 6 = _____

b. 9 + 10 = _____   10 + 9 = _____

c. 17 + 5 = _____   5 + 17 = _____

2. Add. Change the order of the addends. Add again.

a.
```
  30      50
+ 50    + 
```

b.
```
  23      44
+ 44    + 
```

c.
```
  51
+  8    + 
```

d.
```
  82
+ 17    + 
```

3. What do you notice about the sums? _____

> You have discovered the **order property**.

4. Write a statement about order in addition. Use the words **addend** and **sum**.

_____

THINK

Do you think order matters in subtraction? Give an example to support your conclusion.

0-7424-2882-6 *Using the Standards—Algebra*

Name _____ Date _____

Grouping Numbers

Directions: Find different ways to add.

Use colored cubes in different colors to arrange 7   9   4 in different ways.

1. Show three different ways below.

2. You can group numbers different ways to add them. Find the sums. The ( ) tell you which numbers to add first.

   a. (7 + 9) + 4   **b.** 7 + (9 + 4)

   16 + 4   7 + 13

   The sum is _____   The sum is _____

3. Fill in the blanks to finish each addition two ways.

   a. (5 + 8) + 3   **b.** 5 + (8 + 3)

   _____ + 3   5 + _____

   The sum is _____   The sum is _____

4. What do you notice about the sums?   _____

5. Write a sentence or two about grouping the addends in addition.

   _____

DO MORE

Choose three numbers. Use ( ) to show two ways you can group the numbers. Then find the sum in two ways.

0-7424-2882-6 *Using the Standards—Algebra*

Name _____ Date _____

Make It Easy

Directions: Look for an easy way to add.

1. Write the number in the box. Then write the sum.

   a. 3
           9
        + 7 ▷ ☐

   b. 5
           4
        + 5 ▷ ☐

   c. 9
           9
        + 1 ▷ ☐

2. What was done to make each problem easy? _____

3. Group to make sums of 10. Find the sum.

   a. 6
           3
           7
        + 4

   b. 1
           8
           2
        + 9

   c. 4
           5
           6
        + 5

THINK

Make up an addition example that has four addends and a sum of 20. Tell an easy way to do it.

0-7424-2882-6 *Using the Standards—Algebra*

Name _____ Date _____

Adding Odds and Evens

Directions: Tell whether the numbers you are adding are even or odd. Then, see what happens to the sums.

1. Add **evens to evens**. Do three problems. Then, make up your own.

    a.   32   **b.**   92   **c.**   26   **d.**

         + 62   + 4   + 10

2. What do you notice? Write a rule.

    The sum of two _____ numbers is always _____.

3. Add **odds to odds**. Do three problems. Then make up your own.

    a.   11   **b.**   73   **c.**   7   **d.**

         + 7   + 25   + 21

4. What do you notice? Write a rule.

    The _____ of two _____ numbers is always _____.

5. Add **evens and odds**. Do three problems. Then make up your own.

    a.   13   **b.**   24   **c.**   17   **d.**

        + 35   + 15   + 30

6. What do you notice? Write a rule.

    The _____ of an _____ and an_____ number is always _____.

THINK

Why do you think you get these results for the sums?

0-7424-2882-6 *Using the Standards—Algebra*

Name _____ Date _____

Subtracting Odds and Evens

Directions: What do you predict will happen when you subtract evens and odds? Complete the subtractions to find out.

1. Subtract **evens from evens**. Do three problems. Then make up your own.

   a.   38
          − 6

   b.   64
          − 42

   c.   418
          − 102

   d.

2. What do you notice? Write a rule.
   The difference of two _____ numbers is always _____.

3. Subtract **odds from odds**. Do three problems. Then make up your own.

   a.   27
          − 7

   b.   93
          − 41

   c.   85
          − 43

   d.

4. What do you notice? Write a rule.
   The _____ of two _____ numbers is always _____.

5. Subtract **evens and odds**.
   a. Write two problems to subtract odd numbers from even numbers.

   b. Write two problems to subtract even numbers from odd numbers.

6. Write a rule about subtracting even and odd numbers.

THINK

What do you think will happen when you subtract 2 from any number? Will the result be even or odd? Explain.

51

Name _____ Date _____

Related Operations

Directions: Addition and subtraction are related. Look at the examples to discover how.

1. Add or subtract.

a. 4   9   **b.** 8   17
  $+\ 5$ $-\ 5$ $+\ 9$ $-\ 9$

c. 25   75   **d.** 34   42
  $+\ 50$ $-\ 50$ $+\ 8$ $-\ 8$

e. 71   89   **f.** 314   341
  $+\ 18$ $-\ 18$ $+\ 27$ $-\ 27$

2. Describe how addition and subtraction are related.

3. Here are some addition problems. Find the sums. Write the related subtraction problems.

a. 12   **b.** 67
  $+\ 13$ $+\ 21$

4. Here are some subtraction problems. Find the differences. Write the related addition problems.

a. 25   **b.** 88
  $-\ 12$ $-\ 67$

DO MORE

Make up your own problems to show how addition and subtraction are related. Give two examples starting with addition problems. Give two examples starting with subtraction problems.

0-7424-2882-6 *Using the Standards—Algebra*

Name _____ Date _____

Fact Families

You can use the numbers 6 and 2 to make four related facts.

Add.   Change the order.   The four number facts are a
                                        fact family.

```
   6                2
 + 2              + 6
 ---              ---
   8                8
```

Then write the related subtractions.

```
   8                8
 - 2              - 6
 ---              ---
   6                2
```

6 + 2 = 8

2 + 6 = 8

8 - 2 = 6

8 - 6 = 2

Directions: Use two-color counters. Write fact families.

1. Toss 10 counters
    Numbers: _____   Fact Family: _____

2. Toss 17 counters
    Numbers: _____   Fact Family: _____

3. Toss 21 counters
    Numbers: _____   Fact Family: _____

4. Take a handful of counters and toss them
    Numbers: _____   Fact Family: _____

5. Finish these fact families. Write three more facts.

    a. 49 – 19 = 30 _____ _____ _____

    b. 27 + 14 = 41 _____ _____ _____

THINK

When will a fact family have two instead of four facts?

0-7424-2882-6 *Using the Standards—Algebra*

Name _____   Date _____

The Special Number 0

Directions: Work the problems to find out what is special about 0.

1. Add 0.

   a. $9 + 0 =$ _____   **b.** $0 + 15 =$ _____   **c.** $23 + 0 =$ _____

   d. 250   **e.**   0   **f.**   0
        $+ \ 0$ $+ 120$ $+ \ 94$

2. What happens when you add 0 to a number? _____

3. Subtract 0.

   a. $9 - 0 =$ _____   **b.** $8 - 0 =$ _____

   c. 48   **d.** 100
        $- \ 0$ $- \ 0$

4. What happens when you subtract 0 from a number? _____

5. Which picture shows the special property of 0? Circle the picture. Then write two number facts about the picture.

   a.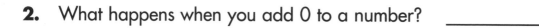

   b.

   c.

DO MORE

Draw a picture that shows addition or subtraction with 0.

0-7424-2882-6 *Using the Standards—Algebra*

Name _____ Date _____

Chart It–Addition

Directions: Use the chart to show what you know about addition properties.

row ⟶

+	0	1	2	3	4	5	6	7
0	0	1	2	3	4	5	6	7
1	1	2	3	4	5	6	7	8
2	2	3	4	5	6	7	8	9
3	3	4	5	6	7	8	9	10
4	4	5	6	7	8	9	10	11
5	5	6	7	8	9	10	11	12
6	6	7	8	9	10	11	12	13
7	7	8	9	10	11	12	13	14

column ↑

1. Use the addition chart. Find a number in the top row. Find a number in the left column. The place where that row and that column cross is the sum.
a. Practice finding a few sums. Write two addition facts you found.

_____   _____

b. Color the row that shows the sums when you add 0.

c. Color the column that shows the sums when you add 0.

d. Put your finger on any number 7 in the chart. Look up along the column and left along the row. What two numbers do you find? Write the numbers.

2. How many fact families can you find using the number 7 as sum? Write them all.

_____

THINK

Why are there not 7 different fact families for the sum 7?

0-7424-2882-6 *Using the Standards—Algebra*

Name _____ Date _____

Missing Addends

Directions: Use what you know about fact families to solve problems.

1. Leanne has 8 dinosaur stickers. Parker gave her some more. Now she has 17 stickers.

How many stickers did Parker give her?   8 + how many more? = 17

8 + _____ = 17

This is a **missing addend**.

a. _____ is the sum. 8 is one addend. The other addend is missing.

b. Use the related facts in a fact family to find the missing addend. What number is missing? _____

2. Jose baked some cookies. Jessica gave him 12 more cookies. Now he has 36 cookies. How many did he start with?

a. Explain what you need to find. _____

b. Use related facts. Find the missing addend.
☐ + 12 = 36   What number is missing? _____

3. Fill in the missing addends.

a. 25 + _____ = 35   **b.** 13 + _____ = 27   **c.** 99 + _____ = 105

d. _____ + 41 = 53   **e.** _____ + 71 = 78   **f.** _____ + 275 = 300

DO MORE

Make up two more word problems about missing addends. Have a friend solve them.

0-7424-2882-6 *Using the Standards—Algebra*

Name _____ Date _____

Tricky Rabbits

Directions: Here are some tricky rabbits.
There are hidden numbers under the rabbits.
Rabbits dressed the same are hiding the same number in the
magic square.

In a magic square,
the sum of each row, each column,
and each diagonal is the same.

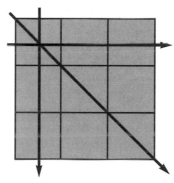

This magic square has sums of 15.

1. Find the numbers the rabbits are hiding.

a. 🐰 = _____

b. 🐰 = _____

c. 🐰 = _____

d. 🐰 = _____

🐰	🐰	8
9	5	🐰
🐰	7	6

🐰	7	6
9	5	🐰
🐰	🐰	8

2. Explain how you found the answers.

DO MORE

What is different about the first square and the second square?
What is the same? What do you think will happen if you exchange
two of the columns?

Name _____ Date _____

Know Your Symbols

Directions: Symbols tell you something.
These are math symbols: >   <   =   +   −   53

1. Choose the correct symbol.

   a. Write the symbol that says **is less than**. _____

   b. Write the symbol that says **plus**. _____

   c. Write the symbol that says **fifty three**. _____

   d. Write the symbol that says **is equal to**. _____

These are different kinds of math symbols. □ ○ ⬭
Sometimes the symbols stand for numbers like 1, 2, 3 . . .
Sometimes the symbols stand for operation signs like + or −.
Sometimes the symbols stand for other signs like >, <, or =.
Use math symbols in **number sentences** like these:

$$6 + 5 = 11 \qquad 6 + 5 > 10 \qquad 6 + 5 < 15$$

2. Tell what the symbol stands for in each sentence.

   a. $6 + \boxed{} = 11$

   b. $6 + 5 \bigcirc 12$

   c. $6 \bigcirc 5 = 10 + 1$

   d. $12 \bigcirc 6 + 6$

THINK

In problem 2, which was the easiest math sentence to solve? Why?

0-7424-2882-6 *Using the Standards—Algebra*

Name _____ Date _____

More Symbols

1. Replace the ◯ with >, <, or =.

   a. 15 ◯ 3 + 5   **b.** 1 + 4 ◯ 4 + 0

   c. 10 − 3 ◯ 3 + 10   **d.** 17 + 2 ◯ 20 − 1

2. Replace the ☐ with a number that makes the number sentence true.

   a. 14 + ☐ = 14   **b.** 3 + 7 = ☐ + 1

   c. 35 − ☐ = 5   **d.** 20 − 17 − 10 − ☐

3. Replace each ◯ with + or − to make the number sentence true.

   a. 15 ◯ 5 = 10   **b.** 33 ◯ 11 = 40 + 4

   c. 9 = 19 ◯ 10   **d.** 6 + 3 + 14 = 30 ◯ 7

4. Write a number sentence with a missing number. Use ☐ . Have a friend solve it.

   _____

5. Write a number sentence with a missing operation sign. Use ◯ . Have a friend solve it.

   _____

THINK

☐ + ☐ = 12 This problem has the same symbol twice. The answer needs to have the same number twice. What is the answer? Explain how you know.

0-7424-2882-6 *Using the Standards—Algebra*

Name _____ Date _____

Make a Code

Directions: Each number stands for a letter in this code. Can you find the rule?

1	3	5	7	9	11	13						
A	B	C	D	E	F	G	H	I	J	K	L	M
N	O											

1. Describe how the code is created.

2. Finish the alphabet. Write the rest of the code in the boxes.

3. Write your name using the code.

4. Write a short message using the code. Have a friend figure out your message.

5. Make up a code using even numbers.

A	B	C	D	E	F	G	H	I	J	K	L	M
N	O											

6. Write your name using your code.

7. Write a different message using the code. Have your friend figure out the message.

THINK

When might people use a code? Do you think this code is easy or hard to figure out? How might you make it harder?

 0-7424-2882-6 *Using the Standards—Algebra*

Name _____ Date _____

Balancing Act

Directions: Look at the pictures. Use math symbols. Write a number sentence to tell about each picture.

1.

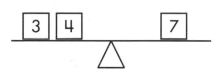

_____

2.

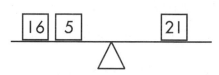

_____

3.

_____

4.

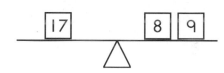

_____

5.

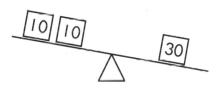

_____

6.

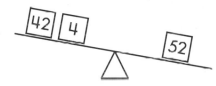

_____

7.

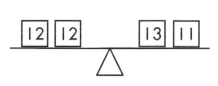

_____

8.

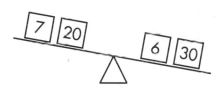

_____

9. What would the weight on the right have to be to balance this scale? _____

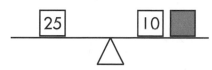

THINK

What number could be on the block to make this balance scale right? Is more than one number possible? Explain your thinking.

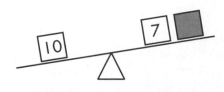

   0-7424-2882-6 *Using the Standards—Algebra*

Name _____ Date _____

More Than One Number

Directions: Sometimes more than one number makes a number sentence true. Look for pairs of numbers to solve the following problems.

1. Replace the symbols with numbers. Find four different pairs of numbers that make this statement true.

   a. △ + ♥ = 11

     △ = ___   ♥ = ___   △ = ___   ♥ = ___

     △ = ___   ♥ = ___   △ = ___   ♥ = ___

   b. Describe how you found the numbers.

2. Replace the symbols with numbers. Find four different pairs of numbers that make each statement true.

   a. ◇ + ♣ = 7

     ◇ = ___   ♣ = ___   ◇ = ___   ♣ = ___

     ◇ = ___   ♣ = ___   ◇ = ___   ♣ = ___

   b. ☐ − ♥ = 1

     ☐ = ___   ♥ = ___   ☐ = ___   ♥ = ___

     ☐ = ___   ♥ = ___   ☐ = ___   ♥ = ___

THINK

Look back at the sentences in problem 2. Can you find more whole numbers that make **a** true or more that make **b** true? Tell why you think so.

     0-7424-2882-6 *Using the Standards—Algebra*

Name _____ Date _____

More and More Numbers

Directions: Read the number sentences. Make each sentence true.

1. Circle the sign that makes the number sentence true.

    a. 13 + 21   >   <   =   34   **b.** 13 + 21   >   <   =   33

    c. 13 + 21   >   <   =   32   **d.** 13 + 21   >   <   =   35

    e. 13 + 21   >   <   =   36   **f.** 13 + 21   >   <   =   37

2. Find five numbers that make each number sentence true.

    a. $7 + 14 > \diamondsuit$ **b.** $32 - 20 < \triangle$

    $\diamondsuit$ = _____ $\triangle$ = _____

    $\diamondsuit$ = _____ $\triangle$ = _____

    $\diamondsuit$ = _____ $\triangle$ = _____

    $\diamondsuit$ = _____ $\triangle$ = _____

    $\diamondsuit$ = _____ $\triangle$ = _____

3. Find two numbers that make each number sentence true.

    a. $\heartsuit + 2 > 54$ **b.** $17 - \square < 12$

    $\heartsuit$ = _____ $\heartsuit$ = _____ $\square$ = _____ $\square$ = _____

DO MORE

Write a number sentence using > that has many solutions. Then write one using < that has many solutions.

        0-7424-2882-6 *Using the Standards—Algebra*

Name _____ Date _____

Missing Digits

Directions: Find the digit that replaces each symbol. It must be a 0, 1, 2, 3, 4, 5, 6, 7, 8, or 9.

1. 3■
+ 7 2
‾‾‾‾
7 8

What digit does ■ have to be? _____

Why? _____

2. 5■
+ 2■
‾‾‾‾
7 8

What digit does ■ have to be? _____

Why? _____

3. 5▲
+ 2▼
‾‾‾‾
7 8

Find ▲ and ▼ .

Is there one answer or more than one answer? _____

▲ = _____ and ▼ = _____   ▲ = _____ and ▼ = _____

▲ = _____ and ▼ = _____   ▲ = _____ and ▼ = _____

▲ = _____ and ▼ = _____   ▲ = _____ and ▼ = _____

▲ = _____ and ▼ = _____   ▲ = _____ and ▼ = _____

4. What if ▲ + ▲ = 6? Can you find one answer for problem 3 now? _____

▲ = _____ and ▼ = _____

5. What if ▲ + ▼ = ▲ ? Can you find one answer for problem 3 now? _____

▲ = _____ and ▼ = _____

DO MORE

Find the answer to problem 3 if ▲ + ▲ + ▼ = 10. Explain how you do it.

0-7424-2882-6 *Using the Standards—Algebra*

Name _____ Date _____

Going Buggy

Directions: Each insect stands for a different number. Find the number for each insect.

1. 🐛 + 🐛 = 6   🐛 = _____

🐞 + 🐞 + 🐞 + 🐞 + 🐞 = 20   🐞 = _____

So 🐛 + 🐞 = _____

2. 🐝 + 🐝 = 10   🐝 = _____

🐝 + 🐜 = 🐝   🐜 = _____

So 🐞 + 🐝 = _____

3. 🕷 + 🕷 + 🕷 = 21   🕷 = _____

🕷 + 1 = 🦋   🦋 = _____

So 🕷 + 🦋 = _____

4. Look at what your symbols mean.

    a. What is 🐛 + 🐝 + 🐞 ?   _____

    b. What is 🕷 – 🐝 ?   _____

DO MORE

Make up your own addition or subtraction problems using these insects. Make up you own animal pictures for missing numbers.

     0-7424-2882-6 *Using the Standards—Algebra*

Name _____ Date _____

Toy Store

puppet 9¢   jigsaw puzzle 12¢   building set 23¢   toy car 18¢

Directions: You are at this toy store. Circle the number sentence that you can use to answer the questions.

1. You have 13¢. How much more do you need to buy a building set?

   a. $13 + 23 = \boxed{}$ **b.** $13 - \boxed{} = 23$ **c.** $13 + \boxed{} = 23$

2. You have a quarter. You buy the toy car. How much change do you get?

   a. $25 - 18 = \boxed{}$ **b.** $25 + 18 = \boxed{}$ **c.** $25 + \boxed{} = 18$

3. You buy a puppet and a jigsaw puzzle. How much do you spend?

   a. $9 + 18 = \boxed{}$ **b.** $9 + 12 = \boxed{}$ **c.** $12 - 9 = \boxed{}$

4. You spend exactly 41¢. What two things do you buy?

   a. $\square + \triangle = 41$ **b.** $\square - \triangle = 41$ **c.** $\square + \triangle < 41$

5. You want to spend less than 31¢. What two things can you buy?

   a. $\square + \triangle = 31$ **b.** $\square - \triangle > 31$ **c.** $\square + \triangle < 31$

THINK

Make up a word problem about buying three things. Write a number sentence using $\square$ $\triangle$ and $\heartsuit$ that can be used to find the answer to your problem.

0-7424-2882-6 *Using the Standards—Algebra*

Name _____ Date _____

Find Your Way

Directions: Follow the directions to find your
way to places on the map.
→ 2 means take 2 steps to the right
← 2 means take 2 steps to the left
↑ 2 means take 2 steps up
↓ 2 means take 2 steps down

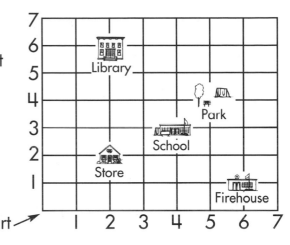

1. Find the start. Follow the directions. Write where you end up. Go back to the start for the next one.

   a. → 4 ↑ 3 _____   **b.** → 2 ↑ 6 _____   **c.** → 5 ↑ 4 _____

2. Use an arrow and number to show how you get from the start to the store.

3. Use an arrow and number to show how you get from the start to the firehouse.

4. You start at the park. You go ← 3 and ↓ 2.
   Where do you end up? _____

5. You start at the library. You go ↓ 5 and → 4.
   Where do you end up? _____

THINK

Put a star on the place where your house could be. Use an arrow and a number to show how to get from the start to your house. Now tell how to get to your house from the school.

0-7424-2882-6 *Using the Standards—Algebra*

Name _____ Date _____

Create Your Own Problems

1. Write an example to show how grouping can help you add three numbers.

2. Write a rule for what happens when you add 1 to any odd number.

3. Show how related operations can help you check a subtraction problem.

4. Write a fact family. Explain how each fact is related to one of the other facts.

5. Write a number sentence using $\bigcirc$ for + or −. Then write what $\bigcirc$ must be to make the sentence true.

6. Make up two number sentences in which < or > is missing. Then show the solutions.

7. Write an equation using two different symbols that has more than one solution.

0-7424-2882-6 *Using the Standards—Algebra*

Name _____ Date _____

Check Your Skills

1. Use ( ) to show two different ways to group numbers in this addition example. Find the sum.

8 + 9 + 7 =   8 + 9 + 7 =

2. Write a fact family using the numbers 13, 6, and 7.

3. Which number sentence has more than one solution? _____

   a. 35 + 3 = ☐   **b.** 35 − 12 = ☐   **c.** 0 + ☐ = ☐

4. Charlie has 75¢. Which number sentence helps you find how much change he gets if he buys the puzzle book? _____

   a. 59 + 75 = ☐   **b.** 59 − ☐ = 75   **c.** 75 − 59 = ☐

5. Find three numbers that make the number sentence true. 40 + ☐ < 50

6.  ♥ + ♥ + 14 = 28   ♥ = _____

7.

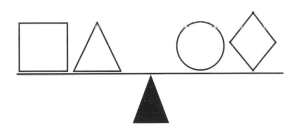

   a. Place these numbers on the scale to balance it.   4   1   8   5

   b. Write an equation to show what you did.

8. Replace the symbol with the correct digit.

$$\begin{array}{r} 7\square \\ +\ 32 \\ \hline 107 \end{array}$$

☐ = _____

     0-7424-2882-6 *Using the Standards—Algebra*

Name _____ Date _____

Picture the Action

Putting together = addition   Taking away = subtraction

Directions: Look at the pictures. Explain the action happening in each picture.
Write **addition** or **subtraction**.

1.

2.

3.

4.

5. Choose one of the equations below and write it next to the picture it describes.
   One of the equations does not have a picture that matches.

   a. $10 - 3 = 7$ **b.** $7 - 3 = 4$ **c.** $5 + 4 = 9$

   d. $5 - 1 = 4$ **e.** $4 + 3 = 7$

DO MORE

Draw a picture for the equation that does not have a picture.

0-7424-2882-6 *Using the Standards—Algebra*

Name _____ Date _____

More Action Pictures

Directions: Look at the pictures. Write **addition** or **subtraction**.

1.

2.

3.

4.

5. Choose one of the equations below and write it next to the picture it describes. One of the equations does not have a picture that matches.

a. $6 + 3 = 9$ **b.** $8 - 3 = 5$ **c.** $6 + 4 = 10$

d. $1 + 3 = 4$ **e.** $3 + 2 = 5$

DO MORE

Make up a word story for the equation that does not have a picture.

0-7424-2882-6 *Using the Standards—Algebra*

Name _____ Date _____

Draw More to Add

12 ◯◯◯◯◯◯◯◯◯◯◯◯
+ 11

Directions: Show how drawing symbols helps you add.

1. Draw more circles to show the addition above. Write the sum.

2. Draw or add symbols for each example. Write the sum.

    a. 21   ●●●●●●●●●●●●●●●●●●●●●
        + 17

    b. 33   xxxxxxxxxxxxxxxxxxxxxxxxxxxxxxxxx
        + 26

    c. 12
        + 13

3. Write the addition example to match the symbols. Find the sum.

    a. ☆☆☆☆☆☆☆☆☆☆☆☆☆☆☆☆☆☆☆☆☆☆☆☆☆
        ☆☆☆☆☆☆☆☆☆☆☆☆☆☆☆☆☆☆☆☆☆☆☆

    b.

DO MORE

Draw symbols to represent an addition problem. Have a friend write the addition example and find the sum.

     0-7424-2882-6 *Using the Standards—Algebra*

Name _____ Date _____

Showing Subtraction

19 ○○○○○○○○○○○○○○○○○○○
−11

Directions: Show how drawing symbols helps you subtract.

1. How can you show subtraction using symbols? _____
    Use Xs to cross out some circles. Write the difference.

2. Draw or cross out symbols for each example. Write the difference.

    a. 45   ● ● ● ● ● ● ● ● ● ●   ● ● ● ● ● ● ● ● ● ●   ● ● ● ● ●
        −21 ● ● ● ● ● ● ● ● ● ●   ● ● ● ● ● ● ● ● ● ●

    b. 29   ▲
        −29

    c. 21
        − 8

3. Write the subtraction example to match the symbols. Find the difference.

    a. ◆ ◆ ◆ ◆ ◆ ◆ ◆ ◆ ◆ ◆ ◆ ◆ ◆ ◆ ◆ ◆ ◆ ◆ ◆ **✗ ✗ ✗ ✗ ✗ ✗ ✗ ✗ ✗ ✗ ✗**

    b. ✶̸
        ✶̸ ✶̸ ✶̸ ✶̸ ☆ ☆ ☆ ☆ ☆ ☆ ☆ ☆ ☆ ☆ ☆ ☆ ☆ ☆ ☆ ☆ ☆ ☆

DO MORE

Draw symbols to represent a subtraction problem. Have a friend write the subtraction example and find the difference.

0-7424-2882-6 *Using the Standards—Algebra*

Name _____ Date _____

Number Talk

There were 18 cupcakes for a party. The children ate 12 cupcakes. How many cupcakes are left?

You use subtraction to tell how many you **take away** or **how many are left**. 18 – 12 = 6

Miss Lee bought 18 donuts. Mr. Garcia bought 12 donuts. How many more donuts did Miss Lee buy?

You use subtraction to tell **how many more**, **how many fewer**, or **compare**. 18 – 12 = 6

Directions: What kind of subtraction does each word problem describe? Circle the **take away** or **compare**. If the problem shows addition, circle **put together**.

1. 24 children chose soccer as a sport.
   15 children chose gymnastics.
   How many more children chose soccer?

   take away
   compare
   put together

2. 24 children chose soccer.
   15 children chose gymnastics.
   How many children chose a sport?

   take away
   compare
   put together

3. 24 children chose soccer.
   15 children dropped out.
   How many children stayed?

   take away
   compare
   put together

4. 24 children chose soccer.
   9 were girls.
   How many were boys?

   take away
   compare
   put together

DO MORE

Ask at least 10 people if they like soccer or gymnastics better. Then write a math problem about your results.

0-7424-2882-6 *Using the Standards—Algebra*

Name _____ Date _____

More Number Talk

Directions: Circle the words that describe the addition or subtraction problem.

1. 19 people at the park buy hotdogs.   **take away**
    9 people at the park buy hamburgers.   **compare**
    How many fewer people buy hamburgers?   **put together**

2. Soccer practice took 55 minutes in all.   **take away**
    Drills took 22 minutes.   **compare**
    How many minutes were spent doing other things? **put together**

3. Leslie practiced piano for 20 minutes on Sunday.   **take away**
    She practiced for 15 minutes on Monday.   **compare**
    She practiced for 10 minutes on Tuesday.   **put together**
    How many minutes did she practice in all?

4. Leslie practiced piano for 20 minutes on Sunday.   **take away**
    She practiced for 15 minutes on Monday.   **compare**
    She practiced for 10 minutes on Tuesday.   **put together**
    How many more minutes did she practice on
    Sunday than on Tuesday?

5. Write the equation and find the answer for each problem 1–4.

    Problem 1: _____   Problem 2: _____

    Problem 3: _____   Problem 4: _____

THINK

Look at problems 3 and 4. What other questions can be asked with the same information? Explain why you can ask many questions.

0-7424-2882-6 *Using the Standards—Algebra*

Name _____ Date _____

Using Cubes

Directions: You can use cubes to show addition and subtraction. Add and subtract with color cubes.

1. The ride has 7 cars that seat two people each and 2 cars that seat four people each. How many cars are there in all?

   How can you use cubes to model the problem? Color the squares to show how you can show 7 + 2.

   ☐ ☐ ☐ ☐ ☐ ☐ ☐ ☐ ☐ ☐ ☐ ☐

2. Explain how the cubes can also show the number sentences with the addends reversed: 2 + 7.

3. Without removing any cubes, how can you use the same cubes to show subtraction?

   a. Describe what you would do to show 9 – 2.

   b. Describe what you would do to show 9 – 7.

4. You found four related facts. What are they called? _____

5. How can you use colored cubes to add three numbers? Color the squares below to show an example.

   ☐ ☐ ☐ ☐ ☐ ☐ ☐ ☐ ☐ ☐ ☐ ☐

DO MORE

How many people can go on the ride at the same time? Find the answer. Tell how you can use cubes to help.

0-7424-2882-6 *Using the Standards—Algebra*

Name _____ Date _____

Using Base-Ten Blocks

Directions: Add and subtract with base-ten blocks.

1. 25
    + 13

    □ 1   ▭ 10   ▦ 100

    a. What do the rods represent? _____
    b. What do the cubes represent? _____
    c. Explain what you do next to add using the blocks.
       Write the sum.

2. 32
    + 29

    a. Explain what you do next to show regrouping in addition using the blocks.
    b. Write the sum.

3. 34
    − 9

    a. Explain what you do next to show regrouping in subtraction using the blocks.
    b. Write the difference.

4. Use base-ten blocks to do each problem.
    a. 46   b. 38   c. 52
        + 26   − 12   − 33

THINK

How is changing a dime to pennies the same as regrouping with rods and cubes?

Published by Instructional Fair. Copyright protected.   0-7424-2882-6 *Using the Standards—Algebra*

Name _____   Date _____

Coloring Blocks

Directions: Use base-ten blocks to add or subtract. Finish each example. Color the blocks to show the answer.

1.   210
       + 95

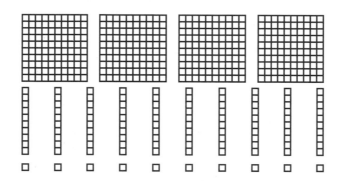

2.   132
       + 149

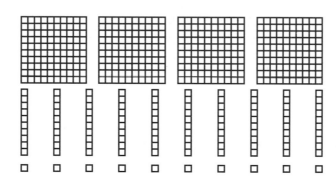

3.   408
       − 79

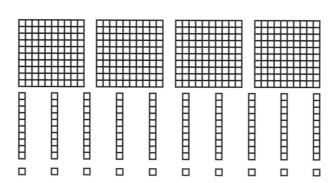

THINK

What figure does do you think ten flats will look like? How many units or cubes is that? Tell how you know.

0-7424-2882-6 *Using the Standards—Algebra*

Name _____ Date _____

Hundred Chart Operations

Directions: Use a hundred chart to add and subtract.

1	2	3	4	5	6	7	8	9	10
11	12	13	14	15	16	17	18	19	20
21	22	23	24	25	26	27	28	29	30
31	32	33	34	35	36	37	38	39	40
41	42	43	44	45	46	47	48	49	50
51	52	53	54	55	56	57	58	59	60
61	62	63	64	65	66	67	68	69	70
71	72	73	74	75	76	77	78	79	80
81	82	83	84	85	86	87	88	89	90
91	92	93	94	95	96	97	98	99	100

1. Put your finger on 3.
Go down the column to count
by tens. Move to the right to
count by ones.

    a. What is 3 + 30? _____

    b. What is 3 + 90? _____

    c. What is 3 + 34? _____

    d. What is 3 + 95? _____

2. Put your finger on 84.
Go up the column to subtract tens.
Move to the left to subtract ones.

    a. What is 84 – 10? _____

    b. What is 84 – 40? _____

    c. What is 84 – 12? _____

    d. What is 84 – 44? _____

3. Use the chart to do each example. Write the answer.

    a.   13
        + 15

    b.   98
        – 64

    c.   59
        + 14

THINK

Explain what you did to find each answer in problem 3.

79

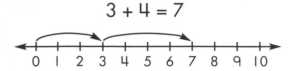

Name _____ Date _____

Number Line Hike

$$3 + 4 = 7$$

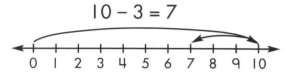

$$10 - 3 = 7$$

You can use a number line to add and subtract.

Directions: This hiking trail looks like a number line. Use the trail to answer the questions. Circle the equation. Write the answer.

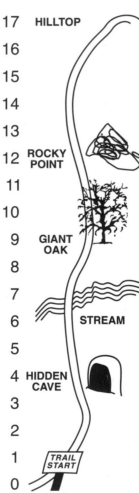

1. Ashley hiked to Hidden Cave. Then, she continued to the stream. How many miles did she hike? _____ miles

$$4 + 2 = \blacksquare \qquad 4 + 0 = \blacksquare \qquad 4 + 6 = \blacksquare$$

2. Devon hiked to the stream. Then he hiked 3 miles more. Where did he end up? _____

$$6 - 3 = \blacksquare \qquad 6 + 3 = \blacksquare \qquad 0 + 9 = \blacksquare$$

3. Carlos hiked to Rocky Point. At the same time, Shayla hiked to Giant Oak.
How far apart were they then? _____ miles

$$12 - 9 = \blacksquare \qquad 12 + 9 = \blacksquare \qquad 12 - 3 = \blacksquare$$

THINK

You hike to Giant Oak. You make one stop on the way. In how many ways can you do it? Write the equations.

0-7424-2882-6 *Using the Standards—Algebra*

Name _____ Date _____

Number Line Hike (cont.)

4. How much closer to the start is Rocky Point than Hilltop? _____ miles

$$12 - 0 = \blacksquare \qquad 17 - 12 = \blacksquare \qquad 12 - 17 = \blacksquare$$

5. Gabe hiked to the end of the trail. Then he hiked to Rocky Point. How many miles did he hike in all? _____ miles

a. $17 - 5 = \blacksquare \qquad 17 + 5 = \blacksquare \qquad 12 + 5 = \blacksquare$

b. Explain how you know this is an addition problem.

6. Felix hiked to the stream. Then he hiked back to the start. Write an equation to show how many miles he hiked in all.

7. Cesar hiked to Hidden Cave. He continue to Giant Oak and then to Rocky Point. Write an equation to show how he hiked and the total number of miles.

8. Write an addition and a subtraction problem about hiking on this trail.

THINK

Draw two number lines that show tens from 0 to 150. Write an equation adding tens and show it on the number line. Write an equation subtracting tens and show it on a number line.

0-7424-2882-6 *Using the Standards—Algebra*

Name _____ Date _____

Create Your Own Problems

1. Describe an event in real life that shows addition.

2. Draw a picture that shows addition.

3. Describe an event in real life that shows subtraction.

4. Draw a picture that shows subtraction.

5. Draw a number of squares and a number of circles. Write an addition sentence and a subtraction sentence.

6. Make up a subtraction example and show it on a number line.

7. Make up an addition example using 3 addends. Show it by coloring in these squares.

0-7424-2882-6 *Using the Standards—Algebra*

Name _____ Date _____

Check Your Skills

I. Circle the equation that describes the picture.

  a. $4 - 2 = 2$ **b.** $2 + 6 = 8$ **c.** $2 + 4 = 6$

2. 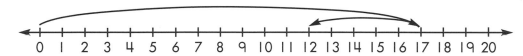   Write the equation that the symbol picture shows.

3. Write the following word problems.

  a. Write a subtraction problem using the words **take away**.

  b. Write a subtraction problem using the word **how many more**.

4. Make up a word problem that can be solved by $25 + 75 =$ ■ .

5. Write the equation shown on the number line.

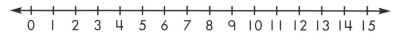

6. $2 + 4 + 7 = 13$ Show how this equation can be represented:

  a. using a number line

  b. using cubes

83

0-7424-2882-6 *Using the Standards—Algebra*

Name _____ Date _____

Changes

Directions: Look at the pictures. What happens? Circle the word that describes the change.

I. The plant grows   **taller**   **shorter**.

2. The carrot gets   **larger**   **smaller**.

3. The balloon gets   **larger**   **smaller**.

THINK

What happens if you blow up a balloon and then let it go? Tell how the size changes.

84

Name _____ Date _____

Changes (cont.)

4. The cat is **higher** **lower**.

5. The bag of popcorn is **fatter** **thinner**.

6. Describe something that gets taller, higher, or larger over time.

7. Describe something that gets shorter, lower, or smaller over time.

THINK

How have you changed since you were 2 years old? Write two sentences to compare some thing about yourself.

0-7424-2882-6 *Using the Standards—Algebra*

Arts and Crafts

Directions: Use comparison words. Answer the questions.

1. Li-san makes a dish with clay. The clay circle was
    5 inches across. Now it is 10 inches across.

    a. Now the clay is _____.

    b. Explain how you chose the comparison word to use.

2. Yolanda makes a shell necklace. Fist she had
    25 shells. Now the necklace has 33 shells.

    a. Now the necklace is _____.

    b. Explain how you chose the comparison word to use.

3. Mrs. Miller pours some paint into each child's jar.

    a. Now the paint in Mrs Miller's jar is _____.

    b. Now the paint in the child's jar is _____.

4. Mrs. Miller taught art for 10 years.

    a. Mrs Miller was _____ then.

    b. Now Mrs. Miller is _____.

DO MORE

Ask an adult about something they learned to do when they were younger. Listen for comparison words.

0-7424-2882-6 *Using the Standards—Algebra*

Name _____   Date _____

Describing Change

Directions: Read the stories. Tell what kind of changes happen. Write the word.

1. A car is going fast. The car is running out of gas. Now it will go

    _____ .

2. In the autumn, the leaves fall from the tree. The number of leaves on the

    tree _____ .

3. It is turning into night. The sky is getting _____ .

4. Your friend LeShawn was born two months before you.

    LeShawn is _____ than you.

5. Write two different sentences about something that changes over time. Use the
    word **larger** in one sentence. Use the word **smaller** in the other sentence.

    a.

    b.

6. Write two different sentences about something that changes over time. Use the
    word **taller** in one sentence. Use the word **shorter** in the other sentence.

    a.

    b.

DO MORE

Think of a pair of opposite words that describe a change. Write a story about
change using your words.

0-7424-2882-6 *Using the Standards—Algebra*

Name _____ Date _____

Draw the Changes

Directions: Draw pictures to show the changes.

1. Two people share a pizza.

   Three people share a pizza.

   Four people share a pizza.

   a. What happens to the size of the each person's slice?

   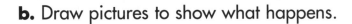

   b. Draw pictures to show what happens.

2. Baby sister is building a tower with blocks.

   She adds some blocks. She adds more blocks.

   a. What happens to the tower?

   b. Draw pictures to show what happens.

THINK

What if the baby adds 1 block, then takes away 2 blocks, and then repeats the pattern? How will the tower change? Explain.

　　　　0-7424-2882-6 *Using the Standards—Algebra*

Name _____ Date _____

Draw the Changes (cont.)

3. The children made a snowman.

The sun shines. It gets warmer and warmer.

a. What happens to the snowman as it melts?

_____

b. Draw pictures to show what happens.

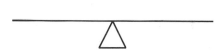

4. The scale is balanced.

Tammy puts a weight on the left.

Josh puts another weight on the left.

a. What happens to the left side of the scale?

_____

b. Draw pictures to show what happens.

5. What would happen to the left side of the scale if Josh removes his weight and then Tammy removes her weight? Explain.

DO MORE

Draw two sets of pictures that show change. Write about the changes.

0-7424-2882-6 *Using the Standards—Algebra*

Name _____ Date _____

In The Garden

Directions: Write the best word to complete each sentence. Match each word with only one sentence.

1. The green peppers get _____.   **taller**

2. The day gets _____.   **redder**

3. The tomatoes get _____.   **hotter**

4. The corn plants get _____.   **longer**

5. The pumpkin vines get _____.   **increases**

6. The number of beans _____.   **larger**

THINK

Which of the things on this page can you compare using numbers?

0-7424-2882-6 *Using the Standards—Algebra*

Name _____   Date _____

How Does Your Garden Grow?

Directions: Which comparison statements make sense? Circle the letter of correct statement in each pair.

1. **a.** The squash is 1 pound heavier this week than last week.
    b. The squash is 10 degrees warmer today.

2. **a.** The temperature is 5 degrees warmer today than it was yesterday.
    b. The temperature is 10 feet longer today.

3. **a.** The tomato is 3 feet longer today than it was yesterday.
    b. The tomato is 1 pound heavier today than it was last week.

4. **a.** The corn stalk grew by 2 feet in one month.
    b. The corn stalk is 25 inches wider than one month ago.

5. **a.** The number of beans increased from 100 to 500.
    b. The number of beans turned redder today than yesterday.

6. **a.** The pumpkin vine grew by 15 degrees.
    b. The pumpkin vine grew 5 feet longer.

7. Choose one of the examples above. Explain why one sentence is wrong and the other is right.

_____

THINK

Name different ways you can use numbers to describe a growing tree.

0-7424-2882-6 *Using the Standards—Algebra*

Name _____ Date _____

Changes You Can Count

Directions: You can use numbers to describe some changes. Look at each picture. Describe the picture without using numbers. Then describe the change with numbers.

1. **a.** What the picture shows:

_____

_____

b. The boy grows _____ inches.

2. **a.** What the picture shows:

_____

_____

b. One swims in_____feet deeper water.

3. **a.** What the picture shows:

_____

_____

b. The car goes _____ miles further.

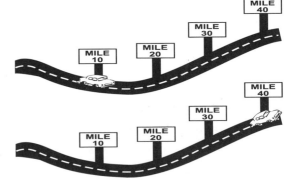

THINK

Describe growing up in two ways: without numbers, and then with numbers.

0-7424-2882-6 *Using the Standards—Algebra*

Name _____ Date _____

Changes You Can Count (cont.)

4.

Inning	1	2	3	4	5	6	7	8	9
Westfield	0	0							
Middlefield	2	6							

a. What changes? _____

b. How is the change measured? _____

c. Middlefield scores _____ more runs.

5. a. What changes?

_____

_____

b. How is the change measured?

_____

c. The bottle has _____ cups less.

6. Draw a picture of something where change can be measured. Show something before and after the change. Use numbers to describe the change.

THINK

You are jumping rope. You keep jumping and jumping. You start fast and then get tired. How can you use numbers to measure the changes in how you jump?

0-7424-2882-6 *Using the Standards—Algebra*

Name _____   Date _____

Temperature Changes

Directions: Temperature is measured in **degrees**. This thermometer says 40 degrees. Color in the thermometers below to show changes in temperature. Write the temperatures below each thermometer.

1. It is getting warmer. Show the temperatures. Write the temperatures.

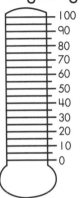   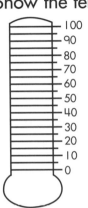   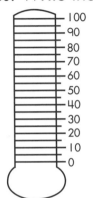   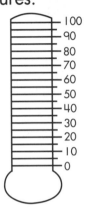

_____   _____   _____   _____

2. It is getting cooler. Show the temperatures. Write the temperatures.

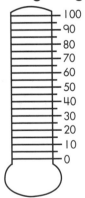   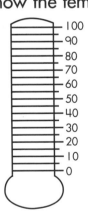   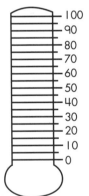

_____   _____   _____   _____

THINK

Tell how many degrees the temperature changed from the first thermometer to the last in example 1. Tell how many degrees it changed in example 2.

0-7424-2882-6 *Using the Standards—Algebra*

Name _____ Date _____

Time Changes

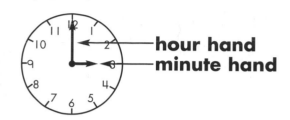

hour hand
minute hand

Directions: This clock says 3 o'clock. How does the time change?

1. It is getting later. Draw hands on the clocks below to show time changes.
    Write the time under each clock.

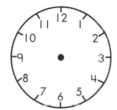 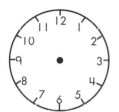 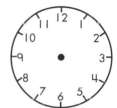 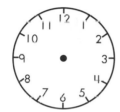

_____ _____ _____ _____

2. Look at these clocks. By how many minutes is time changing? Write the times.

1:35 _____ _____ _____

THINK

How much time passed between the time on the first clock and the time on the last
clock in problem 2? Think of an activity at home or school that takes about that time.

0-7424-2882-6 *Using the Standards—Algebra*

Name _____ Date _____

United States Flag

The U.S. flag has 13 stripes. The stripes represent the original 13 colonies. The stars represent the number of states in the union. Today's flag has 50 stars because there are 50 states.

Directions: Look at the pictures of flags. Look at the chart. Answer questions about how the flag changed.

Year	1777	1795	1818	1846	1861	1908	1948	1960
Number of stars	13	15	20	28	34	46	48	50

Betsy Ross Flag, 1777

1795

1846

1861

1908

1960 (current flag)

1. What changed on the flags? _____

2. What remained the same? _____

3. Write two sentences about flags. Use numbers in your comparison statements.

THINK

In 1818, there were three different arrangements for 20 stars. Draw a picture of different ways you think the stars could have been arranged.

0-7424-2882-6 *Using the Standards—Algebra*

Name _____ Date _____

United States Flag (cont.)

4. How many more stars were on the 1795 flag than on the 1777 flag? _____

5. How many more stars were on the 1861 flag than on the 1846 flag? _____

6. How many fewer stars were on the 1846 flag than on the 1948 flag? _____

7. If you made a graph of the number of stars on each date, would you see a larger change between 1777 and 1861 or between 1861 and 1960?

_____

Explain how you found your answer. _____

8. Find out how many students are in your class. Create a class flag with symbols to show that many students. Show how your flag would change if you had 3 more students.

THINK

Suppose the United States added 10 more states every 50 years from 1777 until now. How many stars would be on the flag today? Begin with 13 stars in 1777.

0-7424-2882-6 *Using the Standards—Algebra*

Name _____ Date _____

You Decide

Directions: Solve these problems about change. Assign reasonable numbers to
the change.

I. The children line up in size places. The second child is 40 inches tall.

    a. Write possible numbers for the number of inches under each picture.

_____ inches   _____ inches   _____ inches   _____ inches

    b. Explain how you decided on the numbers.

2. The price of a computer monitor went down each year. The lowest price is
$175. The highest price was $500.

    a. Write possible prices for each year.

1993   1996   1999   2002   2004

$____ $____ $____ $____ $____

    b. Explain how you decided on the numbers.

    c. By how much did the price of the monitor change from 1990 to 2004?

THINK

Make up a question using the information in problem 1. Make up another question
about change that can be asked using the information in problem 2.

    0-7424-2882-6 *Using the Standards—Algebra*

Name _____ Date _____

A Snowy Week

Directions: Look at the graph. Answer the questions about the changes in snow amounts.

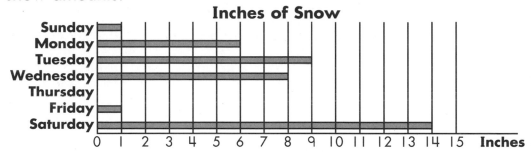

Inches of Snow

1. Look at the snow that fell between Sunday and Tuesday.

   a. Describe the change between Sunday and Monday using numbers.

   _____

   b. Describe the change between Monday and Tuesday using numbers.

   _____

2. Look at the snow that fell between Tuesday and Thursday.

   a. Describe the change between Tuesday and Wednesday using numbers.

   _____

   b. Describe the change between Wednesday and Thursday using numbers.

   _____

3. Look at all the changes between one day and day after. Between which two days is there the greatest change? Describe the change using numbers.

   _____

THINK

Be a weather reporter! Write three or more sentences to tell about the snowy week. Be sure to use lots of number facts. Make a graph to show how the amount of snow grew.

99

Name _____ Date _____

Eating Contest

Directions: At the carnival, there was a burrito eating contest. Read the results from the pictograph. Answer the questions.

Burritos Eaten	
Big Al	🫔 🫔 🫔 🫔 🫔 🫔 🫔
Little Lucy	🫔 🫔 🫔 🫔
Marty the Mouth	🫔 🫔
Eat 'Em Up Ed	🫔 🫔 🫔 🫔
Hungry Hal	🫔 🫔 🫔 🫔 🫔

🫔 = 2 burritos

1. Who won the contest? _____ won by eating _____ burritos.

2. How many more burritos did the fastest eater eat than the slowest eater? _____

3. Which two people ended up in a tie? _____

4. The results show how many burritos each person ate in 10 minutes. If the time had been shorter, would people eat more or fewer burritos? _____

5. If the contest ran for 20 minutes, how many burritos do you think Hungry Hal would eat? _____ Explain your thinking. _____

6. In 5 more minutes, Al and Lucy and Marty eat 2 more burritos each. Ed and Hal eat 8 more each.
   a. Add symbols to the pictograph to show the new results.
   b. Who wins the contest now? _____
   c. Who would be tied? _____

THINK

What other kinds of contests can you think of? Tell what is measured to find the winner.

0-7424-2882-6 *Using the Standards—Algebra*

Name _____ Date _____

Collecting Shells

Directions: Gina collects shells. She began in 1998. How long will this hobby last?
Use the data to finish making the bar graph. Answer the questions.

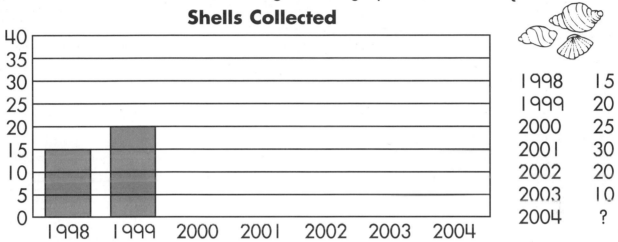

1998	15
1999	20
2000	25
2001	30
2002	20
2003	10
2004	?

1. Finish the graph.

2. What changes do you see in the number of shells collected between 1998 and 2001? Describe the change in numbers. _____

3. Write the pattern from 1998 to 2001. _____ _____ _____ _____

4. If the pattern continued, how many shells would Gina collect in 2003? _____

5. The pattern changed after 2001. How did the number of shells collected change after 2001? Describe the change using numbers. _____

6. Write the pattern from 2001 to 2003. _____ _____ _____

If the pattern continues, how many shells will Gina collect in 2004? _____

DO MORE

Survey some students about how their collections changed over time. Make a graph of the results for one collection.

0-7424-2882-6 *Using the Standards—Algebra*

Name _____ Date _____

Changes in Area

Area is the space that something covers.
The shaded area is 1 square unit.

Directions: Count the number of shaded squares
to find the area. Tell about the changes.

1. a. _____ square units

b. _____ square units

c. Describe the changes. _____

d. By how much did the area change? _____ square units

2. a. _____ square units

b. _____ square units

c. Describe the changes. _____

d. By how much did the area change? _____ square units

3.

a. Describe the changes in words. _____

b. Describe the changes using numbers. _____

THINK

What pattern does the area in example 3 show? Use grid paper to shade the next
area in the pattern.

0-7424-2882-6 *Using the Standards—Algebra*

Name _____ Date _____

Geoboard

Directions: Use a geoboard. Make shapes.

Draw pictures of what you do.

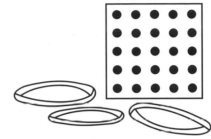

1. Make three shapes that show increasing areas.

2. Make three shapes that show areas that increase by 3 square units.

3. Make three shapes that show areas that decrease by 2 square units.

THINK

Describe how you made the pattern of growing areas in example 2.
What would the next area in your pattern be?

0-7424-2882-6 *Using the Standards—Algebra*

Name _____ Date _____

Making Cookies

Rosa makes cookies and decorates them by hand. She can finish 1 cookie each minute. The Sweet Factory makes and decorates cookies by machine. The factory can finish 6 cookies a minute.

Directions: Look for patterns to measure the changes in the number of cookies finished each minute.

Rosa	1	2	3			
Sweet Factory	6	12	18			
Faster Factory	10					

1. Rosa makes _____ more cookies each minute. The number of cookies Rosa finishes forms a pattern. Fill in the table for Rosa's cookies.

2. The Sweet Factory makes _____ more cookies each minute. The number of cookies the Sweet Factory finishes forms a pattern. Fill in the table for the Sweet Factory's cookies.

3. How many cookies will the factory finish in the time it takes Rosa to finish 6 cookies? _____ cookies

4. How many cookies will Rosa finish in the time it takes the factory to finish 42 cookies?
   a. _____ cookies
   b. Explain how you found your answer.

5. Faster Factory can finish 10 cookies each minute.
   a. Fill in the table for Faster Factory.
   b. How many cookies will Faster Factory finish in the time it takes Rosa to finish 50 cookies? _____ cookies

THINK

Write a comparison question that can be answered by using the table on this page.

0-7424-2882-6 *Using the Standards—Algebra*

Name _____ Date _____

Guess the Rule

Directions: Compare the IN numbers and OUT numbers.

Complete the table. Write the rule.

1.

IN	OUT
0	3
1	4
2	5
3	
4	
5	

Rule: The OUT number is _____ more than the IN number.

2.

IN	OUT
0	4
2	6
4	8
6	
8	
10	

Rule: The OUT number is _____ more than the IN number.

3.

IN	OUT
20	15
19	14
18	13
17	
16	
15	

Rule: The OUT number is _____ less than the IN number.

4.

IN	OUT
10	7
11	8
12	9
13	
14	

Rule: The OUT number is _____ less than the IN number.

THINK

Make up your own rule. Put the numbers in a table. Ask a friend to guess the rule.

0-7424-2882-6 *Using the Standards—Algebra*

Name _____ Date _____

Make a Table

Directions: Fill in the tables to match each rule. Choose your own IN numbers.

1. **Rule:** The OUT number is 10 more than the IN number.

IN	OUT

2. **Rule:** The IN number plus 5 equals the OUT number.

IN	OUT

3. **Rule:** The IN number − 2 equals the OUT number.

IN	OUT

4. **Rule:** The OUT number is 100 more than the IN number.

IN	OUT

THINK

You can use symbols to stand for the changing numbers.

Rule: □ − 1 = △   when □ stands for the IN number
△ stands for the OUT number

Choose numbers and fill in this table.

IN	OUT

0-7424-2882-6 *Using the Standards—Algebra*

Name _____ Date _____

Create Your Own Problems

1. Draw three pictures that show something that grows longer over a period of time.

2. Tell about some sport. Give number facts that can be used to show a change.

3. Describe a change that happens in one of the seasons.

   a. Describe the change without using numbers.

   b. Describe the change using numbers.

4. Create a pictograph or bar graph that shows change.

   Tell what changes it shows.

5. Write a math word problem about the change in temperature. Color in the temperatures and label.

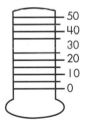 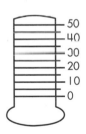

_____ _____

6. Ask ten people to name their favorite TV show. Write a math problem about your results.

7. Make up a rule for a Guess the Rule table. Fill in the table with numbers that show your rule.

0-7424-2882-6 *Using the Standards—Algebra*

Name _____ Date _____

Check Your Skills

1. Write **higher** or **lower**.

   a. An airplane is about to land. It is getting _____.

   b. It is raining. You left a pail outdoors. The water in the pail gets _____.

2. Write the correct comparison word.

   a. Look at the worm.

     It crawls toward the leaf. It is getting _____ to the leaf.

   b. Look at Ginny's fingernails.

     They are growing _____.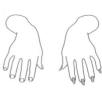

3. Write a word problem about change that involves money. The answer should be "$3 more."

4. Look at the graph.

   Tell how many more inches of rain there was in April than in March. _____ inches

5. Draw two pictures. Show Marisa as 5 inches taller than Lynda.

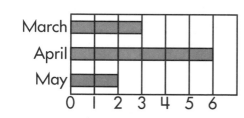

6. Fill in the table to show the change from IN numbers to OUT numbers.

IN	24	20	16	12	8
OUT	19	15			

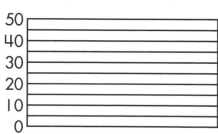

108

Posttest

1. Study the exercise pattern.

    a. Describe the pattern in words.

    b. Circle the kind of pattern.   **growing**   **repeating**

    c. Use the letters A, B, and C to write a matching pattern. _____

2.   1   5   9   13

    a. Explain how the number pattern is created.

    b. Write the next two numbers. _____ _____

3. Jessica is taller than Clara. Ben is taller than Jessica. Shawn is shorter than Ben and Clara. Write the names in order from shortest to tallest.

_____ _____ _____ _____

4. Describe the rule for sorting these cards.

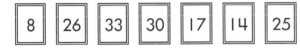

5. Draw the next three shapes.

6. Use the picture to write a fact family. _____

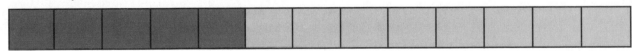

7. Use ( ) to show how grouping can help you add these three numbers. Write the example and the sum. Explain what you do.   43   8   22

    0-7424-2882-6 *Using the Standards—Algebra*

Posttest (cont.)

8. Gabriella bought her dog a 12-inch dog bone. Now the bone is 9 inches long. Circle the number sentence can you use to find out how much the dog ate.

a. $9 + 12 = \square$ **b.** $12 + \square = 9$ **c.** $12 - 9 = \square$

9. Write >, < , or = to make each sentence true.

a. $14 \bigcirc 42$ **b.** $20 + 10 \bigcirc 10 + 20$

10. Look at the picture of the flower.

a. Draw a shorter flower on the left.
b. Draw a flower that is 2 inches taller on the right.

11. Write the number that makes the sentence true. $54 + \square = 60 + 4$

12. Find three numbers than make the sentence true. $25 > 18 + \square$

_____   _____   _____

13. Find the value of ♥ + $\square$.

♥ $+ 3 = 7$ ♥ $=$ _____ $7 + \square = 19$ $\square =$ _____

♥ $+ \square =$ _____

14. Write an equation to show what happens in the picture.

     0-7424-2882-6 *Using the Standards—Algebra*

Answer Key

Pretest 7–8
1. **a.** triangle, triangle, square
   b. repeating
   c. triangle
2. **a.** 1, 3, 5, 7, 9, 11
   b. 13
3. **a.** Baseball cap, bike helmet, winter hat should be in one circle; sneaker, clog, slipper, high heel shoe, and skate should be in second circle.
   b. Things you wear on your head; things you wear on your feet.
   Another possible sorting: sports things and other things.
4. even numbers, odd numbers
5. square, circle
6. **a.** $(8 + 2) + 9 = 19$
   b. $54 + (30 + 70) = 154$
7. a
8. **a.** >
   b. <
9. **a.** shorter
   b. longer
10. 6
11. any three numbers from 6, 5, 4, 3, 2, 1, 0
12. 4
13. $9 + 7 = 16$, $7 + 9 = 16$, $16 - 7 = 9$, $16 - 9 = 7$
14. 11, 12

What Belongs? 9
1. dog, cat, bird
2. rope, game, ball
3. banana, hamburger, candy bar
4. Answers will vary.
5. Answers will vary. Possible answers include notebook, pencil, desk, teacher.

Sort and Graph .10
1. **a.** ||||
   b. |||
   c. ||
   d. ⊥⊥⊥⊥
2. Check graph.
3. 5, 4, 3, 2

Alphabet Soup .11
1. C A B J V T W; 7
2. H P S; 3
3. D E K L; 4

Pattern Blocks .12
1. **a.** 2; drawing of parallelogram and triangle
   b. parallelogram, triangle
   c. Answers will vary.
   d. ▱
   e. extend the pattern to 10 blocks
   f. drawing of triangle
2. Answers will vary.

Order It 13
1. drink
2. second or last
3. second or last
4. sunblock, towel, drink, sandals
5. Answers will vary.

Sorting Blocks .14
1. a, b, and c should be sorted by shading, shape, and size, in any order.
2. Answers will vary.
3. a, b, and c should be sorted by shading, shape, and size, in any order.
4. Answers will vary.

Sorting Buttons 15
1. 7, 4, 4
2. 7, 3, 5
3. Answers will vary.

Animal Babies .16
1. 8
2. 5
3. 10
4. 2
5. The pig from problem 3 should be circled.
6. Check graph.
7. 2, 5, 8, 10
8. Answers will vary.

Weather Wise .17
1. **a.** 6
   b. 7
   c. 4
   d. 3
2. 3, 4, 6, 7

0-7424-2882-6 *Using the Standards—Algebra*

Answer Key (cont.)

3. **a.** 0
   b. 1
   c. 3
   d. 0
4. **a.** 0, 1, 3
   b. 0 appears twice

Comparing Numbers 18

1. **a.** <, is less than
   b. =, is equal to
   c. >, is greater than
   d. <, is less than
   e. <, is less than
   f. =, is equal to
2. **a.** and **b.** Answers will vary.
   c. When the same number appears twice

Pennies and Nickels 19

1. N N N P P P P P P
2. P P P P P N N N N N
3. 21
4. 30
5. **a.** and **b.** 21 < 30 and 30 > 21 in either order.

Puzzles 20

1. 10, 20, 30, 40, 50; DANCE
2. 10, 12, 14, 16, 18, 20, 22; TOP MARK

More Puzzles .21

1. 30, 29, 28, 19, 12, 9, 8, 5, 3; MARCH, JULY
2. It is not a pattern. It is not all even numbers.
3. Answers will vary.

Toy Shelf 22

1. toy car facing right is next; Pattern is cars facing right, left, repeating.
2. tiger missing; Pattern shows bear, tiger, bunny, repeating.
3. A book; B sailboat; Pattern is sailboat, book, book, repeating.

Linking Patterns 23

Answers will vary.

Sound It Out 24

1. horn
2. horn
3. drum, bell
4. drum, bell
5. Answers will vary.

Shape Up 25

1. triangle
2. star
3. Answers will vary. Two shapes should repeat.
4. Answers will vary. Three shapes should repeat.
5. large square; size changes
6. shaded heart; shading changes

Patterns in Rows 26

1. **a.** Answers will vary. Possible answer: shaded square followed by 2 unshaded squares, repeating
   b. Answers will vary. Possible answer: unshaded square followed by 2 shaded squares, repeating
   c. Continue pattern in both rows.
2. **a.** Answers will vary.
   b. Continue pattern in both rows.

Make a Quilt 27

1. Answers will vary. Possible answer: shaded square, unshaded square, repeat
2. Answers will vary. Possible answer: X, shaded square, repeat
3. Answers will vary. Possible answer: O, X, repeat
4. Answers will vary. Possible answer: shaded square X, O repeat
5. unshaded square, shaded square, X, repeat
6. Quilt pattern should continue.

Different Ways .28

1. circle, square
2. rectangle, rectangle
3. heart, X
4. triangle, →, →
5. **a.** A A B B A A B B
   b. 4 5 5 4 5 5
   c. 1 1 1 2 1 1 1 2 or A A A B A A A B

Old MacDonald 29

1. E I E I O
2. **a**, **b**, and **c** should be three different numbers.
   d. Using 1, 2, and 3: possible answer is 1 2 1 2 3 1 2 1 2 3
3. here, there, here, there
4. **a**, **b**, and **c** should be three different numbers.
   d. Using 3, 4, and 5: possible answer is 3 3 4 3 3 5 3 3 4 3 3 5

0-7424-2882-6 *Using the Standards—Algebra*

Answer Key (cont.)

1. c
2. a
3. e
4. b
5. d

1. a. 11
   b. 12
   c. 13
   d. 10 + 4 = 14
   e. Each sum is 1 more than the one before.
2. a. 68
   b. 58
   c. 48
   d. 78 – 40 = 38
   e. Each difference is 10 less than the one before.
3. a. 17
   b. 15
   c. 13
   d. 6 + 5 = 11
   e. The first number is 1 less; the second number is 1 less; the sum is 2 less than the one before.

1. a. even
   b. odd
   c. odd
   d. odd
   e. even
   f. even
2. On left side of the street: 86, 98, 100; on right side 67, 79, 193

1. a. $2
   b. Her bank has two more dollars each week.
   c. 9, 11, 13, 15
   d. $11
2. a. $1
   b. $2
   c. The amount added increases by $1 each week.
   d. 11, 16, 22, 29
   e. $16

1. a. 7, 14
   b. 2, 4
   c. 4, 8
2. skip counting by 2s
3. Drawing of 10 smiley faces; 6, 8, 10, 12, 14, 16, 18, 20

1. Check number line.
2. Check number line.
3. Check number line.
4. Check number line.
5. Check number line.

1. a. 50, 55, 60
   b. 50, 55, 60, 65, 70, 75
   c. Yes, because the numbers increase
2. a. No, because the temperatures go up and down with no pattern
   b. Temperatures go down by 5 degrees; no, because the numbers decrease

1. The following boxes should be shaded and the numbers written: 10, 20, 30, 40, 50, 60, 70, 80, 90, 100
2. The following boxes should be shaded and the numbers written: 5, 15, 25, 35, 45, 55, 65, 75, 85, 95
3. The following boxes should be shaded and the numbers written: 3, 13, 23, 33, 43, 53, 63, 73, 83, 93
4. all show patterns of adding 10
5. they start from different numbers

0-7424-2882-6 *Using the Standards—Algebra*

Answer Key (cont.)

Paint Set Patterns . . . . **.38**
1. Filled-in chart shows pads: 1, 2, 3, 4, 5; pencils: 2, 4, 6, 8, 10; brushes: 3, 6, 9, 12, 15; paint jars: 4, 8, 12, 16, 20
2. pads: 1, 2, 3, 4, 5; pencils: 2, 4, 6, 8, 10; brushes: 3, 6, 9, 12, 15; paint jars: 4, 8, 12, 16, 20
3. They all are growing patterns, and the same number is added to get the next number.
4. They start with different numbers and add a different number.
5. The number 12 in the brush row should be circled.

Bubbles, Bubbles Everywhere . . . . **.39**
1. Two more rows of bubbles should show 8 and then 16 bubbles.
2. 1, 2, 4, 8, 16
   a. yes
   b. Each number is double the one before.
   c. 1, 2, 4, 8, 16, 32, 64

Ladybug Diagram . . . . **.40**
1. a. 5
   b. 6
   c. 2
2. dark with spots

Music Diagram . . . . **.41**
1. a. Marie
   b. Elsa, Savio
   c. Joshua
2. a. 1
   b. 2
   c. 1
3.

```
     Flute              Guitar
   (    2    (    2    )    1    )
              Flute and Guitar
```

Pizza Patterns . . . . **.42**
1. a. 11
   b. 5, 7, 9, 11
2. a. 16
   b. 7, 10, 13, 16

Up and Down . . . . **.43**
1. a. 6
   b. 5
   c. 9
   d. 8
   e. 12, 11
2. 6, 5, 9, 8, 12, 11
3. 12, 9, 16, 13, 20, 17
4. Answers will vary.

Create Your Own Problems . . . . **.44**
Answers will vary.

Check Your Skills . . . . **.45**
1. 142, 131, 103, 42, 34
2. a. >
   b. =
3. b
4. circle, heart
5. a. 20, 23; growing
6. 11, 5; repeating
7. A A B C A A B C
8. a. growing
   b. repeating
   c. growing

Order in Your Life . . . . **.46**
1. a. yes
   b. Answers will vary.
2. a. no
   b. Answers will vary.
3. a. no
   b. Answers will vary.
4. a. yes
   b. Answers will vary.

Order in Addition . . . . **.47**
1. a. 14, 14
   b. 19, 19
   c. 22, 22
2. a. 80; 50 + 30 = 80
   b. 67; 44 + 23 = 67
   c. 59; 8 + 51 = 59
   d. 99; 17 + 82 = 99
3. They are the same.
4. Answers can vary but should be similar to: When you change the order of the addends, the sum is the same.

114

Answer Key (cont.)

Grouping Numbers 48
  1. Answers will vary. Shading of 7, 9, and 4 squares should be in three different orders.
  2. **a.** 20
     b. 20
  3. **a.** 13, 16
     b. 11, 16
  4. The sums are the same.
  5. Answers can vary but should be similar to: The sum is the same even if you group the addends in different ways.

Make It Easy 49
  1. **a.** 10, 19
     b. 10, 14
     c. 10, 19
  2. Group numbers to have a sum of 10.
  3. **a.** 20
     b. 20
     c. 20

Adding Odds and Evens 50
  1. **a.** 94
     b. 96
     c. 36
     d. Answers will vary.
  2. even, even
  3. **a.** 18
     b. 98
     c. 28
     d. Answers will vary.
  4. sum, odd, even
  5. **a.** 48
     b. 39
     c. 47
     d. Answers will vary.
  6. sum, even, odd, odd

Subtracting Odds and Evens 51
  1. **a.** 32
     b. 22
     c. 316
     d. Answers will vary.
  2. even, even
  3. **a.** 20
     b. 52
     c. 42
     d. Answers will vary.

  4. difference, odd, even
  5. **a.** Answers will vary.
     b. Answers will vary.
  6. When you subtract an even and an odd number, the answer is always odd.

Related Operations 52
  1. **a.** 9, 4
     b. 17, 8
     c. 75, 25
     d. 42, 34
     e. 89, 71
     f. 341, 314
  2. They are opposites. The sum minus on addend gives the other addend.
  3. **a.** 25; $25 - 13 = 12$
     b. 88; $88 - 21 = 67$
  4. **a.** 13; $13 + 12 = 25$
     b. 21; $21 + 67 = 88$

Fact Families 53
  1–4. Answers will vary.
  5. **a.** $49 - 30 = 19, 30 + 19 = 49, 19 + 30 = 49$
     b. $14 + 27 = 41, 41 - 14 = 27, 41 - 27 = 14$

The Special Number 0 54
  1. **a.** 9
     b. 15
     c. 23
     d. 250
     e. 120
     f. 94
  2. The sum is the same as the other addend.
  3. **a.** 9
     b. 8
     c. 48
     d. 100
  4. The difference is the same as the number you are subtracting from.
  5. c; $5 + 0 = 5, 5 - 0 = 5$

Chart It—Addition 55
  1. Answers will vary.
  2. 4 in all; $0 + 7 = 7, 7 + 0 = 7, 7 - 0 = 7$,
     $7 - 7 = 0$;
     $1 + 6 = 7, 6 + 1 = 7, 7 - 6 = 1, 7 - 1 = 6$;
     $2 + 5 = 7, 5 + 2 = 7, 7 - 5 = 2, 7 - 2 = 5$;
     $3 + 4 = 7, 4 + 3 = 7, 7 - 3 = 4, 7 - 4 = 3$

115

0-7424-2882-6 *Using the Standards—Algebra*

Answer Key (cont.)

Missing Addends **56**
  1. a. 17
  b. 9
  2. a. Answers will vary.
  b. 24
  3. a. 10
  b. 14
  c. 6
  d. 12
  e. 7
  f. 25

Tricky Rabbits **57**
  1. a. 4
  b. 3
  c. 1
  d. 2
  2. Answers will vary.

Know Your Symbols **58**
  1. a. <
  b. +
  c. 53
  d. =
  2. a. 5
  b. <
  c. +
  d. =

More Symbols **59**
  1. a. >
  b. >
  c. <
  d. =
  2. a. 0
  b. 9
  c. 30
  d. 7
  3. a. –
  b. +
  c. –
  d. –
  4. Answers will vary.
  5. Answers will vary.

Make a Code **60**
  1. The odd numbers in order match the letters of the alphabet in order.
  2. 15 = H, 17 = I, 19 = J, 21 = K, 23 = L, 25 = M, 27 = N, 29 = O, 31 = P, 33 = Q, 35 = R, 37 = S, 39 = T, 41 = U, 43 = V, 45 = W, 47 = X, 49 = Y, 51 = Z
  3.–7. Answers will vary.

Balancing Act **61**
  1. 3 + 4 = 7
  2. 16 + 5 = 21
  3. 8 + 4 > 10 or 10 < 8 + 4
  4. 17 = 8 + 9
  5. 10 + 10 < 30 or 30 > 10 + 10
  6. 42 + 4 < 52 or 52 > 42 + 4
  7. 12 + 12 = 13 + 11
  8. 7 + 20 < 6 + 30 or 6 + 30 > 7 + 20
  9. 15

More Than One Number **62**
  1. a. Any four of the pairs: 0, 11; 1, 10; 2, 9; 3, 8; 4, 7; 5, 6; 6, 5; 7, 4; 8, 3; 9, 2; 10, 1; 11, 0
  b. Answers will vary.
  2. a. Any four of the pairs: 0, 7; 1, 6; 2, 5; 3, 4; 4, 3; 5, 2; 6, 1; 7, 0
  b. Any two numbers that vary by 1, such as 7 and 6.

More and More Numbers **63**
  1. a. =
  b. >
  c. >
  d. <
  e. <
  f. <
  2. a. any number less than 21
  b. any number greater than 12
  3. a. any number greater than 52
  b. 6, 17, and any number between 6 to 17

Missing Digits **64**
  1. 6; because 6 + 2 = 8
  2. 4; because 4 + 4 = 8
  3. more than one answer
     0, 8; 1, 7; 2, 6; 3, 5; 5, 3; 6, 2; 7, 1; 8, 0
  4. yes; ▲ = 3, ▼ = 5
  5. yes; ▲ = 8, ▼ = 0

Published by Instructional Fair. Copyright protected.   0-7424-2882-6 *Using the Standards—Algebra*

Answer Key (cont.)

Going Buggy 65
1. 3, 4; 3 + 4 = 7
2. 5, 0; 4 + 5 = 9
3. 7, 8; 7 + 8 = 15
4. **a.** 3 + 5 + 4 = 12
   b. 7 − 5 = 2

Toy Store 66
1. c
2. a
3. b
4. a
5. c

Find Your Way .67
1. **a.** school
   b. library
   c. park
2. →2 ↑2
3. →6 ↑1
4. store
5. firehouse

Create Your Own Problems 68
   Answers will vary.

Check Your Skills 69
1. (8 + 9) + 7 = 24, 8 + (9 + 7) = 24
2. 6 + 7 = 13; 7 + 6 = 13; 13 − 7 = 6; 13 − 6 = 7
3. c
4. c
5. 0, 9, and any number between
6. 7
7. **a.** 8 and 1 on one side of the scale, and 5 and 4
      on the other side
   b. 8 + 1 = 5 + 4
8. 5

Picture the Action 70
1. 5 ducks and 4 ducks coming together; addition
2. There were 10 apples on a tree. Three apples fall
   off; subtraction
3. There were 5 balloons, and one popped;
   subtraction
4. 3 boxes in the truck and 4 moving into the truck;
   addition
5. Picture in #1: c
   Picture in #2: a
   Picture in #3: d
   Picture in #4: e

More Action Pictures 71
1. The flower had 8 petals, but 3 are falling to the
   ground; subtraction
2. 3 tricycles joined 2 tricycles; addition
3. 3 frogs are jumping into the water to join the 6
   frogs; addition
4. The tray holds 6 ice cream cones and 4 ice cream
   sandwiches; addition
5. Picture in #1: b
   Picture in #2: e
   Picture in #3: a
   Picture in #4: c

Draw More to Add 72
1. 11 circles added; 23
2. **a.** 17 dots added; 38
   b. 26 Xs added; 59
   c. 12 symbols beside the 12; 13 symbols beside
      the 13; 25
3. **a.** 28 + 24 = 52
   b. 9 + 14 = 23

Showing Subtraction 73
1. Cross out some symbols; 11 circles crossed out; 8
2. **a.** Cross out 21 circles; 24
   b. Cross out 29 triangles; 0
   c. 21 symbols should be drawn; 8 crossed out; 13
3. **a.** 28 − 12 = 16
   b. 47 − 29 = 18

Number Talk 74
1. compare
2. put together
3. take away
4. compare

More Number Talk 75
1. compare
2. compare
3. put together
4. compare
5. Problem 1: 19 − 9 = 10
   Problem 2: 55 − 22 = 33
   Problem 3: 20 + 15 + 10 = 45
   Problem 4: 20 − 10 = 10

Published by Instructional Fair. Copyright protected.

0-7424-2882-6 *Using the Standards—Algebra*

Answer Key (cont.)

Using Cubes 76

 1. 7 cubes one color and 2 cubes a different color

 2. Look at the cubes left to right and then right to left.

 3. a. Cover 2 cubes.

  b. Cover 7 cubes.

 4. fact family

 5. Use 3 different color cubes; Answers will vary.

Using Base-Ten Blocks 77

 1. a. tens

  b. ones

  c. Put the cubes together and put the rods together; 38

 2. a. Put the cubes together, exchange 10 cubes for 1 rod, and put the rods together; 61

  b. check drawings; 61

 3. a. You cannot take 9 cubes away from 4 cubes, so exchange 1 rod for 10 cubes. Take 9 cubes away from 14;

  b. check drawings; 25

 4. a. 72

  b. 26

  c. 19

Coloring Blocks 78

 1. 305; 3 flats and 5 cubes shaded

 2. 281; 2 flats, 8 rods, and 1 cube shaded

 3. 329; 3 flats, 2 rods, and 9 cubes shaded

Hundred Chart Operations 79

 1. a. 33

  b. 93

  c. 37

  d. 98

 2. a. 74

  b. 44

  c. 72

  d. 40

 3. a. 28

  b. 34

  c. 73

Number Line Hike 80–81

 1. 6; $4 + 2 = 6$

 2. Giant Oak; $6 + 3 = 9$

 3. 3; $12 - 9 = 3$

 4. 5; $17 - 12 = 5$

 5. a. 22; $17 + 5 = 22$

  b. Answers will vary.

 6. $6 + 6 = 12$

 7. $4 + 5 + 3 = 12$

 8. Answers will vary.

Create Your Own Problems 82

  Answers will vary.

Check Your Skills 83

 1. c

 2. $22 - 6 = 16$

 3. Answers will vary.

 4. Answers will vary.

 5. $17 - 5 = 12$

 6. a.

  b.

Changes 84–85

 1. taller

 2. smaller

 3. larger

 4. lower

 5. fatter

 6. Answers will vary.

 7. Answers will vary.

Arts and Crafts .86

 1. a. wider or larger

  b. Answers will vary.

 2. a. longer

  b. Answers will vary.

 3. a. lower or less

  b. higher or more

 4. a. younger

  b. older

Describing Change 87

 1. slower

 2. decreases

 3. darker

 4. older

 5-6. Answers will vary.

0-7424-2882-6 *Using the Standards—Algebra*

Answer Key (cont.)

 1. **a.** decreases or gets smaller
    b.

 2. **a.** gets taller
    b. Two towers of blocks with second one having more blocks than the first. Number of blocks will vary.
 3. **a.** melts, get smaller
    b. Two snowmen, second one smaller than the first.
 4. **a.** goes down
    b.

 5. The left will move up until the scale is balanced again.

 1. larger
 2. hotter
 3. redder
 4. taller
 5. longer
 6. increases

 1. a
 2. a
 3. b
 4. a
 5. a
 6. b
 7. Answers will vary.

 1. **a.** Child grows taller
    b. 2
 2. **a.** The person on the right is swimming in deeper water than the person on the left.
    b. 2
 3. **a.** Car is driving farther and farther.
    b. 30
 4. **a.** score
    b. runs
    c. 4

 5. **a.** level of the liquid
    b. cups
    c. 2
 6. Answers will vary.

 1. Answers will vary, but increasing temperatures should be shown.
 2. Answers will vary, but decreasing temperatures should be shown.

 1. Answers will vary, but later times should be shown.
 2. 1:40; 1:45; 1:50

 1. number of stars and arrangements of stars
 2. number of stripes and the colors
 3. Answers will vary.
 4. 2
 5. 6
 6. 20
 7. 1777 to 1861; Answers will vary.
 8. Answers will vary.

 1. **a.** Answers will vary, but numbers should show an increasing pattern with 40 for the second child.
    b. Answers will vary.
 2. **a.** Answers will vary but should show a decreasing pattern for $500 to $175.
    b. Answers will vary.
    c. $325

 1. **a.** 5 inches more
    b. 3 inches more
 2. **a.** 1 inch less
    b. 8 inches less
 3. Friday and Saturday; 14 inches more

 1. Big Al, 14
 2. 10
 3. Lucy and Ed
 4. fewer
 5. Answers will vary.
 6. **a.** Graph should be extended to show 1 more symbol each for Al, Lucy, and Marty, and 4 more symbols each for Ed and Hal.
    b. Hungry Hal
    c. Al and Ed

 0-7424-2882-6 *Using the Standards—Algebra*

Answer Key (cont.)

Collecting Shells 101
1. Check graph.
2. increases; 5 more shells collected each year
3. 15, 20, 25, 30
4. 40 shells
5. the number collected decreased; 10 fewer shells collected each year
6. 30, 20 10; 0

Changes in Area 102
1. a. 2
   b. 5
   c. larger area
   d. 3 more square units
2. a. 16
   b. 12
   c. smaller area
   d. 4 fewer square units
3. a. Each area is larger than the one before.
   b. Areas increase from 1 to 4 to 9 square units.

Geoboard 103
1.–3. Answers will vary.

Making Cookies 104
1. 1; 4, 5, 6
2. 6; 24, 30, 36
3. 36
4. a. 7
   b. extend both patterns
5. a. 10, 20, 30, 40, 50, 60
   b. 500

Guess the Rule 105
1. 6, 7, 8; 3
2. 10, 12, 14; The OUT number is 4 more than the IN number.
3. 12, 11, 10; The OUT number is 5 less than the IN number.
4. 10, 11; The OUT number is 3 less than the IN number.

Make a Table .106
1.–4. Answers will vary.

Create Your Own Problems 107
Answers will vary.

Check Your Skills 108
1. a. lower
   b. higher
2. a. closer
   b. longer
3. Answers will vary. Possible answer: Alice has $7. Chad has $10. How much more does Chad have?
4. 3
5. Answers will vary. Check that one drawing is 5 inches taller on the graph.
6. 11, 7, 3

Posttest 109–110
1. a. Answers will vary.
   b. repeating
   c. A B C A B C
2. a. Add 4 to the number to get the next number.
   b. 17, 21
3. Shawn, Clara, Jessica, Ben
4. All the odd numbers are together. All the even numbers are together.
5. square, circle, circle
6. $8 + 5 = 13, 5 + 8 = 13, 13 - 5 = 8, 13 - 8 = 5$
7. $43 + (8 + 22); 43 + 30 = 73$; Answers will vary.
8. c
9. a. <
   b. =
10. a. Drawing of shorter flower on the left.
    b. Drawing of flower 2 inches taller on the graph on the right.
11. 10
12. Any number less than or equal to 6.
13. 4; 12; 16
14. $12 - 3 = 9$

0-7424-2882-6 *Using the Standards—Algebra*

sum	tally marks
difference	addends
bar graph	pictograph

Published by Instructional Fair. Copyright protected.

0-7424-2882-6 *Using the Standards—Algebra*

sets of lines drawn to show how many

the answer to an addition problem

$7 + 12 = 29$

$$\begin{array}{r} 7 \\ +\,12 \\ \hline 29 \end{array}$$

the number you add in an addition problem

$7 + 12 = 29$

the answer to a subtraction problem

$25 - 12 = 13$

$$\begin{array}{r} 25 \\ -\,12 \\ \hline 13 \end{array}$$

a graph that uses pictures to show how many

Favorite Flavor
Vanilla
Chocolate
= 2 children

a graph where the lengths of the bars shows how many

Favorite Flavor
9
8
7
6
5
4
3
2
1
0
Vanilla
Chocolate

0-7424-2882-6 *Using the Standards—Algebra*

fact family

area

repeating pattern

growing pattern

grouping property

order property

0-7424-2882-6 *Using the Standards—Algebra*

the amount of space inside a shape—measured in square units

10 square units

related addition and subtraction facts

$5 + 6 = 11$ $11 - 6 = 5$
$6 + 5 = 11$ $11 - 5 = 6$

a series of numbers that get larger using a rule

3   6   9   12   15
Rule: Add 3

two or more things repeat according to a rule.

A B A B A B

The order of the addends does not change the sum.

$3 + 4 = 4 + 3$

The way the addends are grouped does not change the sum.

$3 + (4 + 1) = (3 + 4) + 1$

0-7424-2882-6 *Using the Standards—Algebra*

zero (0) property	even numbers
odd number	**number sentence**
equation	**digit**

0-7424-2882-6 *Using the Standards—Algebra*

a number of things that can be grouped in 2s with none left over

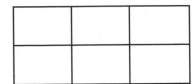

6 is even

The sum of zero and any number is the same as the other addend.

$5 + 0 = 5$ $12 + 0 = 12$
$0 + 8 = 8$ $0 + 51 = 51$

a sentence using numbers and math symbols instead of words

$5 + 5 = 10$
$5 < 6$
$6 - 1 > 0$

a number of things that has one left over when grouped in twos

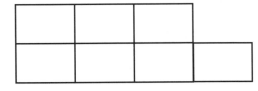

7 is odd

the symbols 0, 1, 2, 3, 4, 5, 6, 7, 8, and 9 used in other numbers

2-digit numbers: 12, 54, 60, 93
3-digit numbers: 340, 100, 725, 999

a number sentence with an equal (=) sign

$3 + 7 = 8 + 2$

0-7424-2882-6 *Using the Standards—Algebra*

number line

skip counting

operation sign or symbol

balance scale

temperature

thermometer

0-7424-2882-6 *Using the Standards—Algebra*

counting by 2s, 5s, 10s or other numbers to form a pattern

2, 4, 6, 8, 10, ...
5, 10, 15, 20, ...
10, 20, 30, 40, ...

line with equally spaced marks used to show operations

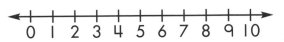

an instrument that weighs two things

symbol that tells what you do with the numbers to solve a problem

+ tells you to add
− tells you to subtract

an instrument that measures how hot or cold something is

the measure of how hot or cold something is

0-7424-2882-6 *Using the Standards—Algebra*